THE
REALIZATION
AND
SUPPRESSION
OF
THE
SITUATIONIST
INTERNATIONAL

an
annotated bibliography
1972 — 1992

Simon Ford

Copyright Simon Ford 1995.

First Published in 1995 by
    AK Press   AK Press
    22 Lutton Place   P.O. Box 40286
    Edinburgh, Scotland   San Francisco, CA 94140-0286
    EH8 9PE   USA

Printed in Great Britain by BPC Wheatons Ltd. Exeter

British Library Cataloguing in Publication Data

Realization and Suppression of the
Situationist International : Annotated
Bibliography, 1972 — 1992
   I. Ford, Simon
   016.7009045

   ISBN 1-873176-82-1

Library of Congress Cataloguing-in-Publication Data

Ford, Simon 1965-
   The realization and suppression of the situationist international
: an annotated bibliography, 1972 — 1992,
     p. cm.
   Includes bibliographical reference and index.
   ISBN 1-873176-82-1 : $10.95
   I. Internationale situationniste. 2. Arts, Modern--20th century--
Europe. 3. Avant-garde (Aesthetics)--Europe--History--20th
century. I. Title
NX542.F68 1994
016.7--dc20   94-25741
     CIP

Book design and lay out donated by Freddie Baer.

TABLE OF CONTENTS

ACKNOWLEDGEMENTS

This bibliography has been very much a collaborative effort. Many people have given up their time and expertise and encouraged me in the completion of the project. In particular I would like to thank Stewart Home, Richard Turner, and Ramsey Kanaan. Thanks are also due to the following for readily offering advice and information; Freddie Baer, Bob Black, Ken Knabb, Lucy Forsyth, Natasha Held, Chris McKay, Cynthia Morrison-Bell, George Robertson, Barry Pateman, David Haden, and David Bell. I would also like to thank the staff at the National Art Library, Victoria and Albert Museum, for all their support and guidance.

The bibliography relied extensively on the references contained in many of the publications cited. The most important of these were the works by Mirella Bandini, Gerard Berreby, Per Hofman Hansen, Stewart Home, Ken Knabb, Thomas Y Levin, Greil Marcus, Sadie Plant, Roberto Ohrt, Jean-Jacques Raspaud and Jean-Pierre Voyer, and Peter Wollen.

ABBREVIATIONS

Bd.	Band [Volume]
B.M.	British Monomark
CA.	California
C.R.Q.S.	Centre de recherche sur la question sociale
ed(s).	editor(s)
F.O.	For Ourselves
hbk.	hardback
I.C.A.	Institute of Contemporary Art
ill.	illustrated
ISBN	International standard book number
ISSN	International standard serial number
M.I.T.	Massachusetts Institute of Technology
n.d.	no date
OCLC	Online Computer Library Center
p.	page.
pbk.	paperback
pp.	paginated page(s).
S.I.	Situationist International
S.l.	sine loco (If no place or probable place can be given)
s.n.	sine nomine (If the name of the publisher is unknown)
t.p.	title page

CHRONOLOGY OF KEY PUBLICATIONS

1972   Raspaud, Jean-Jacques and Jean-Pierre Voyer. *L'Internationale situationniste: chronologie, bibliographie, protagonistes (avec un index des noms insultés)*. Paris: Éditions Champ Libre.
Debord, Guy and Sanguinetti, Gianfranco. *La véritable scission dans l'Internationale*. Paris: Éditions Champ Libre.
Vaneigem, Raoul. *The revolution of everyday life*. London: Practical Paradise.

1973   Horelick, Jon. (ed.). *Diversion 1*. New York: Diversion.

1974   Gray, Chris. *Leaving the Twentieth Century: the incomplete work of the Situationist International*. London: Free Fall Publications.

1975   Internationale situationniste. *Internationale situationniste 1958-1969*. Paris: Éditions Champ Libre.
Censor [Gianfranco Sanguinetti]. *Rapporto veridico sulle ultime possibilità di salvare il capitalismo in Italia*. Milan: Ugo Mursia.
Jacobs, David and Winks, Christopher. *At Dusk: the Situationist movement in historical perspective*. Berkeley: Perspectives.

1976   Knabb, Ken. (ed.). *Bureau of Public Secrets 1*. Berkeley: Bureau of Public Secrets.

1977   Bandini, Mirella. *L'estetico il politico: da Cobra all'Internazionale Situazionista, 1948-57*. Rome: Officini Edizioni.

1978   [Wise, Dave.] *The end of music*. Glasgow: Box V2.
Debord, Guy. *Oeuvres cinématographiques complètes*. Paris: Éditions Champ Libre.

1979   Debord, Guy. *Préface à la quatrième édition italienne de 'la société du spectacle.'* Paris: Éditions Champ Libre.
Vaneigem, Raoul. *Le livre des plaisirs*. Paris: Encre.

1981   Knabb, Ken. (ed.). *Situationist International anthology*. Berkeley: Bureau of Public Secrets.

1983   Cronin, Issac and Seltzer, Terrel. *Call it sleep*. London: B.M. Combustion.

1984   Vague, Tom. The 20th century and how to leave it: the boy scout's guide to the Situationist International. *Vague*. (16/17), 1984, pp. 13-46.

1985 Berreby, Gerard, (ed.). *Documents relatifs à fondation de l'Internationale situationniste: 1948-1957*. Paris: Allia.

1987 Ball, Edward. The great sideshow of the Situationist International. *Yale French Studies*. (73), Nov. 1987, pp. 21-37.
Barrot, Jean. *What is situationism?: critique of the Situationist International*. London: Unpopular Books.

1988 Home, Stewart. *The assault on culture: utopian currents from Lettrisme to Class War*. London: Aporia Press and Unpopular Books.
Debord, Guy. *Commentaire sur la société du spectacle*. Paris: Éditions Champ Libre.

1989 Blazwick, Iwona, (ed.). *An endless adventure.... an endless passion... an endless banquet: A Situationist scrapbook*. London: I.C.A. and Verso.
Marcus, Greil. *Lipstick traces: a secret history of the twentieth century*. London: Secker & Warburg.
Martos, Jean-François. *Histoire de l'Internationale situationniste*. Paris: Éditions Gérard Lebovici.
Sussman, Elizabeth, (ed.). *On the passage of a few people through a rather brief moment in time*. Boston: M.I.T. Press; Institute of Contemporary Art, Boston.

1990 Ohrt, Roberto. *Phantom Avant Garde: Eine Geschichte der Situationistischen International und der modernen Kunst*. Hamburg: Edition Nautilus, Galerie van de Loo.
Debord, Guy. *Comments on the society of the spectacle*. London: Verso.
Dumontier, Pascal. *Les situationnistes et Mai 68*. Paris: Éditions Gérard Lebovici.

1991 Debord, Guy. *Panegyric: volume 1*. London: Verso.

1992 Plant, Sadie. *The most radical gesture: the Situationist International in a postmodern age*. London: Routledge.
Viénet, René. *Enragés and Situationists in the Occupation Movement, France, May '68*. London: Autonomedia; Rebel.
Debord, Guy. *Society of the spectacle and other films*. London: Rebel Press.
Debord, Guy. *In girum imus nocte et consumimur igni*. London: Pelagian Press.

INTRODUCTION

This introductory section will not repeat any neat and concise history of the Situationist International. The familiar type of beginning, "The S.I. was formed in 1957 ...", is superfluous here. Instead, this introduction takes for granted the reader's basic awareness of the facts about the group's history and deals specifically with situating the S.I. first within an artistic context, then within a 'publishing' context. The history of the S.I. illustrates a process that has its source in a few cases of obscure self-promotion and its finale in a bibliography of this size.

The schism of 1962, between what has been described as the artistic faction and the political faction, is often cited as the key moment for the group. Although it is significant, there is no evidence to suggest that the remaining 'Debordist' S.I.[1] (in distinction to the Second Situationist International) gave up the fundamental avant-gardist concerns that provided the motivation for their initial formation in 1957. They continued to involve themselves in cultural contestation and even their anti-art stance is a traditional role for the avant-garde and thus still easily assimilated into an artistic context. The 1962 split occurred because Debord and his collaborators had a more ambitious role for the group than that envisaged by Heimrad Prem and the German and Scandinavian sections. This role was revolutionary and would be compromised by too active an engagement in the art world. This being said, it is often overlooked that the only exhibition where the S.I. exhibited as a group took place after the split, in June of 1963, at Odense. This occasion also provided the opportunity for the publication of an important text[2] in which Debord dealt specifically with his vision of the S.I.'s relationship to cultural production.

The S.I.'s continued involvement in film is also overlooked by those trying to promote a post-artistic perspective. Debord often described himself as a film maker[3] and cinema is obviously one of the central art forms of this century. Debord's and René Viénet's continued commitment to film indicates the 'Debordist' S.I. never really excluded the possibility of producing cultural aftefacts.[4] It is also possible to argue that the S.I.'s supposedly most triumphal moment, the events of May '68, are characterized by cultural interventions, manifested in their use of slogans, graffiti, posters and comic strips. The dominance of their work in these fields, over their more overtly political 'interventions', is reflected in the bibliography, which in turn reveals that the majority of the debate concerning their work has taken place in the cultural sphere.

What the S.I. did was to skilfully combine the artistic with the political and the theoretical. They synthesized many of the past strategies of the avant-garde and brought to the realm of cultural discourse a theoretical rigour rarely seen before. As such, they were part of the period between 1945 and 1975 that saw art gradually absorbed by theory, until, for some, only theory was left.[5] This period also saw an attack on the dominance of painting and sculpture and the exploitation of the heritage of Dada. There was a new dissatisfaction with the gallery as a container and frame for art which led to land art, site specific installations and happenings. There was also an attack on art's visuality, an awareness of the commodity status of a work of art, and a growing consciousness of the close relationship between politics and culture.

This period did not necessarily see more theory being produced, rather there was a shift in the status of theory, in the assertion of theory as a potential art work. The following is an editorial introduction to *Art-Language* (1), 1969: "Suppose the following hypothesis is advanced: that this editorial, in itself an attempt to evince some outlines as to what 'conceptual art' is, is held out as a 'conceptual art' work."[6] Theory became a specific form of art practice. The theoretical art work, which did not have to exist outside its description, broke down the separation between art and philosophy and between art objects and interpretation. It is possible to trace a similar development in the S.I., from an art object-based movement to a theory-based movement. The S.I.'s work became constituted almost entirely in text, with the artist metamorphosed into a theorist.[7]

The S.I. has been repeatedly situated in the context of the history of a succession of 20th century avant-garde movements. The disbanding of the S.I. in 1972 is often, erroneously, seen as the conclusion of this narrative.[8] The S.I. existed at a time of great activity in the historicising of the avant-garde. Major studies and retrospective exhibitions on the pre-war movements (Futurism, Dada, Russian Constructivism and Surrealism) had a great influence on their post-war emulators. The S.I. developed a critique of the avant-garde that negotiated, and attempted to resolve, much of the criticism radicals made against these earlier movements.[9] They still, however, saw themselves as a vanguard, as an avant-garde movement. One of their enduring characteristics is a consistent identification with the ideals of avant-gardism, even though Debord criticised the avant-garde for being as specialised and alienated as any other aspect of spectacular culture. By being neither exclusively political theorists nor artists they aimed to escape this co-option into the world of spectacular separation.

The S.I. were pushed towards an extreme position that increasingly denied the possibility of Situationist art in the here and now. For the time being the political realm was appropriated into the artistic realm. The S.I. aesthetised politics of the left wing variety through the absorption and appropriation of an intractable political discourse and bureaucracy into its very structure of organization. The S.I.'s purity was maintained through expulsions, statutes, congresses, and a strict recruitment policy. Many of the pages of the journal are taken up with questions of organization.[10] The S.I. was a typical avant-garde group, and thus the organization was a 'work' in itself, something where all the individual components were subsumed under the ideals of the group. As an evolving work any discordant features that surfaced were removed, and this constituted the group's dynamic driving force. The methods employed, as identified by Wollen, borrowed much from the classic Leninist characteristics of "establishing a central journal, issuing manifestos and agitational leaflets, guarding the purity of the group, and expelling deviationists."[11] The organization had to be limited in size and did not court disciples: "the S.I. can only be a Conspiracy of Equals, a general staff that *does not want troops ... We will only organize the detonation:* the free explosion must escape us and any other control forever."[12] Vaneigem summed this up further in a neat encapsulation of the avant-gardist's dream: "We will form a small, almost alchemical, experimental group within which the realization of the total man can be started."[13] They also went so far as to state that their organization and its propaganda should be seen in the context of the strategy of détournement and thus read as a form of artistic production.

> "Thus the signature of the situationist movement, the sign of its presence and contestation in contemporary cultural reality (since we cannot represent any common style whatsoever), is first of all the use of détournement ... But we should also mention in this context the S.I.'s very forms of 'organization' and propaganda."[14]

The S.I. were experts and specialists of avant-gardism at just the time of the death (or the discourse of the death) of the avant-garde. They can also be read as an attack on this avant-garde tradition, but this attack can itself also be read as part of the tradition. This fundamental problem for the avant-garde was there at its christening:

> "... in the military's traditional lexicon the avant-garde is an elite and expendable shock troop; it attacks with such intensity that it often destroys itself on the enemy's lances, serving in death as a bridge for the army that follows it. But in modern usage the enemy against which culture sends out its avant-garde is itself. The avant-garde is the vanguard of the army it attacks."[15]

The avant-garde, and the Situationists in particular, were very aware of the processes of legitimation and adept at strategies involving publicity, myth-making, self-historification and subversion. These processes have been repeated throughout this century and revolve around the legitimatizing institutions of the media, galleries, museums, and the education system. Its main material manifestation is the production of text in the form of publications or publicity.

The Bibliography

This bibliography has been produced to assist inquirers in discovering the existence and determining the identity of books or other documentary material which may be of interest to them. Other aims were to illustrate how historical processes and critical reception acted upon the S.I. and to chart the spread of this discourse. The bibliography is an effective format in which to achieve this.

Another justification for producing the bibliography, particularly the pro-situationist ('pro-situ') sections, is that many commentators on the S.I. are unaware of the rich culture of 'underground' publishing currently taking place in both the UK and the USA. This sector's contribution to the dissemination of both information and myths concerning the S.I. has had a major effect on the field, especially in the seventies and early eighties. In addition to this historicising role some of these 'marginals' have also attempted to continue where the S.I. left off and develop and update the critique of the society of the spectacle even further.

Since 1972 the S.I. has had a very productive death and this book specifically documents a period of transition from relative obscurity to celebrity. It is also an epitaph produced at a moment that heralds a new stage in this afterlife. Everything after 1992 (including this bibliography) will belong to a new period. The concepts, rightly or wrongly identified with them, have now become part of the common language of critical discourse. The number of references continues to grow, as does the number of publications concerning the group.

The S.I. left behind a body of work that has been mined for the last twenty years by a variety of groups and individuals, to varying degrees of comprehension. It is often the case that the S.I. influence is exaggerated, but since the late sixties there had been a nascent 'pro-situ' scene in both Britain and America. The British scene is characterised by such groups as B.M. Combustion, King Mob, Heatwave, Pleasure Tendency, B.M. Blob, Omphalos, Chronos, Surburban Press, and Spectacular Times. The equivalent American scene is characterised by Ken Knabb's long-lasting Bureau of Public Secrets and groups such as Negation, Diversion, Point-Blank!, For Ourselves, Collective Inventions, and Create Situations. Most of these groups never really sustained their enthusiasm or activities beyond a few sporadic publications in the mid to late seventies and the early eighties.

There is, at present, no reliable account of either milieu so their histories remain to be written. The complications that arise when researching these groups begin with their categorisation. Many of them would strongly object to being described as 'pro-situ'. Indeed this label often gives too much credit to the S.I. at the expense of other more obvious influences, such as anarchism and libertarianism. Another issue is that the authors are often wilfully anonymous and this, in addition to the often inadvertent lack of imprint details, leads to severe problems of attribution and dating. The groups involved are also often vehemently antagonistic towards each other. A fact made apparent in the many unreliable accounts and rumours that circulate within the milieu.

Outside of this 'underground' milieu the placing of the S.I. on the contemporary 'mainstream' cultural map can be attributed to a variety of factors including a generalized sixties revival. The media-constructed nostalgia built up around the 1988 anniversary of May '68 reinforced the interest surrounding two books, the first published in 1988 by the 'underground' Stewart Home[16] and the second published in 1989 by the 'mainstream' Greil Marcus.[17] All these factors together further justified the planning and materialization of the large travelling retrospective show of 1989 (Paris, London, Boston). The S.I. provided an attractive subject for the media so there was no holding back the flood of commentators wishing to have their say. What was previously an area of knowledge holding little interest suddenly became a mark of credibility and gradually became buried under an avalanche of anecdote, exegesis, and opinion, but still little considered examination.[18]

Types of Publication

The following section briefly notes specific types of publishing that constitute the prime material, the documentation, from which the history of the S.I., and by extension the avant-garde, is constructed and disseminated.

The S.I. like most avant-gardes needed the metropolitan centres as an arena for their activities. The city provided access to publicity, communication systems, and a vast audience to support activities. The Paris based S.I. identified four types of publishing; 'state-bureaucratic', 'bourgeois semicompetitive', 'independent' and 'clandestine'. They stated they would use the latter two methods regularly, and 'bourgeois semicompetitive' occasionally (for a "different level of distribution"), but would never use 'state bureaucratic.'[19]

The S.I. recognised that there is no reason why artworks have to precede publications for a movement to have credibility. An example of this is provided by F.T. Marinetti who issued the first manifesto of Futurist painting before any such work existed.[20] This publication of **manifestos** has been a characteristic of 20th century avant-garde movements wishing to articulate programmes, opinions and demands. A manifesto is a public proclamation of an individual's or a group's intentions and beliefs. They are designed to provoke and to stimulate the spectator and employ a rhetorical strategy that minimizes the possibilities for rational considerations. The S.I. recognised them as being the perfect medium for gaining publicity in that they are easily distributed and cheap to produce in large numbers. Whereas books are fundamentally a private experience, the manifesto intervenes in the collective and public domain.[21]

Manifestos can be elaborated upon to form **pamphlets**, the pre-eminent vehicle for the dissemination of S.I. ideas, as they have also been for many radical and anarchist groups. The advantages to be gained from using pamphlets are obvious. They are economical, short, and can be used to react decisively to contemporary events and other publications. Because they are often self published there are rarely any problems with censorship. They are handy and transportable (and disposable).

After the manifesto and the pamphlet the next most useful and popular vehicle for avant-garde discourse is the **periodical**. The periodical can be short-lived, cheap to produce, and is excellent for collecting together diverse opinions. It is quick to react, like the pamphlet, and can respond to the immediate problems of the day. As with the S.I.'s journal, *Internationale situationniste,* an audience is built and developed rather than immediately confronted. Eventually after a few issues you have something that is substantial; something that can be anthologized into a book.

Books have spines, they have an authority and focus that periodicals cannot usually attain. The S.I. did not gain any real notoriety until the late sixties when Debord[22] and Vaneigem[23] published their major treatises. Since then a relatively small amount of books have concentrated on the S.I. exclusively, but this is a state of affairs that is changing. The explosion of interest that erupted in 1988-1989 is in abeyance, but this is being replaced by a much more deeply rooted academic project; books will appear that say more and more about less and less.

Exhibition catalogues extend the effectiveness of an exhibition beyond its fixed location and transmute the temporality of the display into a permanent form. Although it is often cited as the 'kiss of death' for a movement, or an artist, the retrospective exhibition can never actually achieve its main objective, which is the definitive encapsulation and representation of its subject. The retrospective only creates opportunities for more retrospectives.

Exhibitions are also events that can attract the media; they are often reviewed and discussed. The S.I. had a fascinating love/hate relationship with the media. This is apparent in their extensive use of quotations from articles that recorded events that 'illustrated' their theses or mentioned their activities (the more inaccurate the better). The S.I. had an advanced notion of what constituted a successful media strategy. They discovered it is important to stay relatively obscure, not show all your cards at once, spread rumours, drop references, vastly exaggerate your strength, be extreme, and create scandal. An extension of this was the S.I.'s awareness of the value of branding and their zealous protection of their name against 'situation-ism'. Any form of publication or event provides the opportunity for review and publicity. The media is significant because it is an indication of public reaction and therefore a measure of the movement's strength. The press coverage can even become part of the work; two of Debord's books[24] and a film[25] are specifically concerned with reactions from the mass media to his work and activities.

The appearance of a **monograph** on a subject indicates a definite stage in its historification. It is proof of a consensus amongst academic circles, publishers and the art world, that the subject requires such a treatment and that the market is ready for this type of product. This can only occur after the previously mentioned types of material have been produced. A monograph will in turn fuel a further level of research that will examine not only primary source material but also secondary sources, how the movement has been represented by other commentators. The monograph will stimulate the demand for reprints and translations and will soon need revising in the light of new evidence and interpretation. Eventually there is so much material published, in so many forms, that some kind of guide is required to aid the researcher's quest for information.

The **bibliography** appears at this point in a subject's living-death when criticism reaches its critical mass. As such it indicates the death of any innocence in the face of the subject. The weight of material already published and documented will have to be carried by any subsequent writer. This will not, of course, restrict the field of interpretation; the bibliography opens the way for a multiplication of the viewpoints from which the S.I. can be examined.

Criteria Used in the Exclusion and Inclusion of Material

- The bibliography includes published material on the S.I., related groups and individuals published between 1972 and 1992.

- It concentrates primarily on English language publications but also indicates where material has been published in foreign languages.

- Major works that only exist in a foreign language have been included.

- The bibliography also encompasses many reprints and new translations of material originally published before 1972.

- Some of the publications and articles listed have very little information or interpretative value. These are included to represent the breadth of coverage that has occurred.

- The bibliography contains some references to items that I have not personally examined. These have only been included if they originate from a reasonably reliable publication or source.

- The temporal limits (1972-1992) reflect that 1972 was the date of the S.I. disbanding and also the date of the bibliography by John-Jacques Raspaud and Jean-Pierre Voyer.[26] 1992 was selected because of the publication of Sadie Plant's *The most radical gesture*,[27] the 'bitter victory' of the S.I.'s entry into the official culture of institutional curicula and the general disintegration of the field as it enters this next stage.

- All types of publications have been included; features in fanzines, articles in academic journals, newspaper articles, books, sections of books, encyclopedia entries, reprints, anthologies, exhibition catalogues, discussion papers, reviews, pamphlets, posters, manifestos, cassette tapes, videos and films.

- A bibliography can be defined as much by its exclusions as by its inclusions. Conscious omissions include items that only briefly mention the S.I. and items that do not show sufficient S.I. characteristics to be classified as 'pro-situ'. Another area purposely neglected is that of the work of French theorists such as Jean Baudrillard, Gilles Deleuze, Felix Guattari, and Jean-François Lyotard. The connections between the S.I. and the work of these writers has been explored by Plant and countless guides and anthologies already exist on their work. The continental 'pro-situ' scene has been largely ignored because of the obvious research difficulties related to examining material. This problem also relates to material associated with the British and American 'pro-situ' milieus which, because of its often ephemeral nature, is now very rare and thus difficult to examine or even ascertain its existence.

- The annotations aim to summarize and evaluate the items they refer to. They contain quotations in order to either provide a taste of the text's style, summarize the key points, or reproduce a particular piece of significant information. This obviously exposes the item to my editorial interpretation and is thus a problematic but unavoidable practice. The bibliography is only a guide and in no way pretends to fully represent the items described.

Arrangement

Section **1. General Works** refers to predominantly mainstream publications and articles concerning the S.I. as a group.

Section **2. Related Movements** looks at a selection of work on and by the movements that are most closely associated with the S.I. This section contains only introductory texts, predominantly in English.

Section **3. Works on or by Ex-Situationists** collects together work on and by individuals and inevitably reflects the dominance of certain members. English language references have been given priority, as have works published between 1972-92. Where the number of works concerning an individual have not merited a separate section members' activities can be traced through section **9. Index.**

Section **4. American 'Pro-Situs' & Milieu** and **5. British 'Pro-Situs' & Milieu** have been separated from the main body of the bibliography to provide a clearer picture of their particular contributions.

Sections **6. Book Reviews** and **7. 1989 Exhibition Catalogue and Reviews** contains the reviews of the 1989 exhibition and books by Stewart Home and Greil Marcus.

Section **8. Selected Addresses** provides information about where groups and publishers were located. The year given in square brackets refers to the last date I have seen that address used.

Other Sources of Information

This section provides a brief guide to where readers can find out more information or obtain some of the items listed. American and British 'pro-situ' material is not usually available from 'high street' bookshops. The only way of obtaining it is through mail order firms, such as AK Retail, Counter Productions, and A Distribution in Britain and Loompanics Unlimited in America. These distributors produce regular catalogues and can be contacted using the address section. The second most productive avenue is to visit your local anarchist bookshop. In London this would include Freedom Bookshop and Compendium Bookshop both of which have a section devoted to the S.I. Here you can also, occasionally, acquire out-of-print material and foreign language publications. Another method to acquire this material is to visit the annual Anarchist Bookfairs that take place each year around October, in Conway Hall, Red Lion Square, London. Personal contact with the authors and activists themselves may be necessary.

To acquire works actually produced by the S.I. now requires accessing the world of specialist second hand book dealers. In the past there has been S.I. publications appearing in the catalogues of Sam Fogg, Ann Creed and from America, Lure. The post-war avant-garde is becoming a very collectable proposition and this is reflected in the growing number of dealers working in this area. Because of much of this material's ephemeral nature it often disappears, becomes rare, and very collectable. The bibliography can often resemble a shopping list.

The most important public collection of S.I. material is to be found in the Silkeborg Museum, Denmark. This collection was initially built up because of Asger Jorn's connection with the group. There are also many internal documents deposited by the S.I. in l'Institut International d'Histoire Sociale (I.I.H.S) in Amsterdam. In the book *Les situationnistes et Mai 68*[28] Pascal Dummontier lists some of the contents of the I.I.H.S. and also cites the Bibliothèque de Documentation Internationale Contemporaine at Nanterre as holding documents concerning the S.I. Another source at Nanterre is the Bibliothéque universitaire de Nanterre. Many of the publications exhibited in the 1989 exhibition came from the collection of the Musée national d'art moderne, Centre Georges Pompidou, Paris. The most substantial collection of S.I. and 'pro-situ' material in Britain is to be found at the National Art Library, Victoria and Albert Museum, London.

Conclusion

The rather contradictory title of this bibliography is adapted from the S.I.'s description of their attempts at the realization and suppression of art. Its usage here is meant to convey my belief that the S.I. has itself been both realised and suppressed; realised in the sense of its fame; suppressed in the sense that in this fame very little still remains of their initial radical pretensions. This introduction has attempted to situate the S.I. in the context of this century's avant-garde art movements. It has also explored how the S.I. utilized the media and the full range of categories of publications available to them to further their cause. My interest in these particular areas has evidently influenced what has been included and excluded from the bibliography. It has also influenced the choice and arrangement of the sections and effected the content of the annotations. However, this should not distract from what has been a straight forward attempt to collect references and present them in an intelligible and easy-to-use manner. It is this concern that has been the overriding objective of a project that has its roots way back in 1986. Of course, with so much material now available on the group, and its legacy, opinions and interpretations will differ enormously. The following bibliography should help to make these opinions slightly more informed.

Notes

1. A fundamental problem when discussing the S.I. is the question of authorship and responsibility. Although it is obviously problematic to devolve accountability for a movement down to an individual, it is impossible to imagine the S.I. without Guy Debord's contribution. His knowledge and manipulative utilization of the cultural sphere is one of the key factors that enabled the S.I. to survive for so long, in reality and as myth. This is not to downplay the fact that the best of Debord's works were collaborations and produced when he was closely allied with first Michèle Bernstein and Gil J Wolman, then Jorn, Vaneigem, and finally Gianfranco Sanguinetti. His commitment to the S.I. as an organization was also stronger than that of the more individualistic Vaneigem and Jorn.

2. G. Debord, 'The Situationists and the new forms of action in politics or art,' in E. Sussman, ed., *On the passage of a few people through a rather brief moment in time: the Situationist International 1957-1972*, Boston, Mass.: M.I.T. Press; Institute of Contemporary Art, Boston, 1989, pp. 148-153.

3. T. Y. Levin, 'Dismantling the spectacle: the cinema of Guy Debord,' in Sussman, ibid., p. 78.

4. This is Debord in 1970. "Each film could give one or two Situationists working as assistants the opportunity to master their own style in this language; and the inevitable success of our works would also provide the economic base for the future production of these comrades. *The expansion of our audience is of decisive importance.*" Cited in Levin, ibid, p. 77.

5. P. Mann, *The theory-death of the avant-garde*, Bloomington: Indiana University Press, 1991, p. 5.

6. C. Harrison and P. Wood, eds., *Art in theory 1900-1990: an anthology of changing ideas*, Oxford: Blackwell, 1992, p. 873.

7. Debord in the film *La société du spectacle* quotes August von Czieszkowski. "Thus, after the immediate production of art had

ceased to be the most eminent activity and the predicate of eminence has shifted to theory as such, at present it has detached itself from the latter to the extent that there has developed a post-theoretical, synthetic practice whose primary purpose is to be the foundation and truth of both art and philosophy." Cited in Levin, op cit, p. 96.

8. "Thus the S.I. was fated to be incorporated into the legendary series of avant-garde artists and groups whose paths had intersected with popular revolutionary movements at emblematic moments. Its dissolution in 1972 brought to an end an epoch which began in Paris with the 'Futurist Manifesto' of 1909 — the epoch of the historic avant-gardes with their typical apparatus of international organization and propaganda, manifestos, congresses, quarrels, scandals, indictments, expulsions, polemics, group photographs, little magazines, mysterious episodes, provocations, utopian theories, and intense desires to transform art, society, the world and the pattern of everyday life." P. Wollen, in Sussman, op. cit., p. 27.

9. This criticism of past avant-gardes was identified by Debord as an important area for concern in one of the founding papers of the S.I. Here he described the bourgeoisie's attempts to channel all critical and experimental research toward strictly compartmentalized utilitarian disciplines and suppress any "concerted overall critique and research." G. Debord, 'Report on the construction of situations and on the International Situationist tendency's conditions of organization and action,' in K. Knabb, ed., *Situationist International anthology*, Berkeley: Bureau of Public Secrets, 1981, pp. 17-25.

10. See M. Bernstein, 'No useless leniency,' in Knabb, ibid., pp. 47-48; Anon., 'The adventure,' in Knabb, ibid., pp. 60-61; and G. Debord. 'The organization question for the S.I.,' in Knabb, ibid., pp. 298-301.

11. P. Wollen, in Sussman, op. cit., p. 35.

12. Anon., 'The countersituationist campaign in various countries,' in Knabb, op. cit., p. 113.

13. R. Vaneigem, 'Basic banalities II,' in Knabb, ibid., p. 133.

14. Anon., 'Détournement as negation and prelude,' in Knabb, ibid., pp. 55-56.

15. Mann, op. cit., pp. 45-46.

16. S. Home, *The assault on culture: utopian currents from Lettrisme to Class War*, London: Aporia Press and Unpopular Books, 1988.

17. G. Marcus, *Lipstick traces: a secret history of the twentieth century*, London: Secker & Warburg, 1989.

18. A further attraction that could be attributed to the S.I. was the great investment they put into theory. The late eighties was a time when the dominance of theory was suffering something of a backlash and may have been seen to be in need of some historical justification.
19. Anon., 'Sur deux livres et leurs auteurs,' *Internationale situationniste*, (10), p. 70. Translated in Knabb, op. cit., pp. 373-374.
20. Mann, op. cit., p. 6.
21. The First Futurist Manifesto by F.T. Marinetti was published on the front page of *Le Figaro*, a Parisian daily newspaper, on 20 February 1909. Marinetti defined the manifesto's characteristics as violence and precision.
22. G. Debord, *La société du spectacle*, Paris: Buchet-Chastel, 1967.
23. R. Vaneigem, *Traité de savoir-vivre à l'usage des jeunes générations*, Paris: Gallimard, 1967.
24. G. Debord, *Ordures et décombres daballes à la sortie du film "in girum imus nocte et consumimur igni"*. Paris: Éditions Champ Libre, 1982, and G. Debord, *Considération sur l'assassinat de Gérard Lebovici*, Paris: Éditions Gérard Lebovici, 1985.
25. G. Debord, *Refutation of all judgements whether for or against, which have been brought to date on the film "Society of the spectacle"*. Simar Films, 1975. Translated in G. Debord, *Society of the spectacle and other films*, London: Rebel Press, 1992.
26. J. Raspaud and J. Voyer, *L'Internationale situationniste: chronologie, bibliographie, protagonistes (avec un index des noms insultés)*, Paris: Éditions Champ Libre, 1972.
27. S. Plant, *The most radical gesture: the Situationist International in a postmodern age*, London: Routledge, 1992.
28. P. Dumontier, *Les situationnistes et Mai 68: théorie et practique de la révolution (1966-1972)*, Paris: Éditions Gérard Lebovici, 1990. "Le carton K 15/1, à l'I.I.H.S. d'Amsterdam, regroupe une partie des archive et de la correspondence de l'Internationale situationniste, pur la période 1969-1971. Il contient les dosiers suivants: Correspondance scandinave; Conférence 1970; Section italienne; Conférence de Venise 1969; Correspondance américaine 1967-1969; Éditeurs; Débat stratégique; Correspondance avec étrangers; Correspondance américaine 1970; La dernière crise; L'innocence des Olympiens; Correspondance Horelick-Verlaan." — Dumontier, p. 226.

EXPLANATORY NOTE ON THE FORM OF BIBLIOGRAPHICAL REFERENCES.

Book.

Author or editor. *Title*. Place of publication: Publisher, date. Number of pages. International standard book number.

Essay in book or exhibition catalogue.

Author of essay. Title of section. In: Author or editor of book. *Title of book or exhibition catalogue*. Place of publication: Publisher, date. International standard book number: Page numbers of the section.

Article in serial.

Author. Title of article. *Title of periodical*. Volume (part or number), date, page numbers. International standard serial number.

1. GENERAL WORKS ON THE S.I.

1.

Apostolidès, Jean-Marie. Du Surréalisme à l'Internationale situationniste: la question de l'image. *Modern Language Notes*. 105 (4), 1990, pp. 727-749.

Translates as 'From Surrealism to the Situationist International: the question of image'. Contents; I.1 Le champ de l'imaginaire, I.2 Espace et temps du surréalisme, I.3 Production et circulation des images, I.4 La production imaginaire, II.1 L'IS et la critique du spectacle, II.2 L'IS et la question du temps, II.3 Les diverses formes du spectaculaire, II.4 La pratique situationniste, III.1 Vers une économie de l'imaginaire, III.2 Le capital imaginaire. Text in French.

2.

Ball, Edward. The great sideshow of the Situationist International. *Yale French Studies*. (73), Nov. 1987, pp. 21-37, ill.

An extensive essay organised under the following chapters; 'Sire, I am from the other country', 'The Situationists do Paris', 'The great show of reification', 'Détournement and the Postmodern', and 'The society of the Situationist'. Ball is chiefly concerned with situating Situationist techniques and theory in the context of recent postmodern developments but he also provides a useful introductory guide.

3.

Ball, Edward. 'The beautiful language of my century': from the Situationists to the Simulationists. *Arts Magazine*. 63 (5), Jan. 1989, pp. 65-72, ill.

Ball draws on the relationship between the Situationist's project and contemporary art; specifically that of Gordon Matta-Clark, Daniel Buren, Cindy Sherman, Laurie Simmons, Haim Steinbach, Louise Lawler, and Allan McCollum. "Edward Ball is a researcher in the critical division of K&B Art, a New York partnership." — editorial. A French translation of this text also appeared as; La belle langue de mon siècle. *Art Press*. (France), (134), March 1989, pp. 27-32, ill.

4.

Bandini, Mirella. *L'estetico il politico: da Cobra all'Internazionale Situazionista, 1948-57*. Roma: Officini Edizioni, 1977. 391 p., [16] p. of plates, ill. (Saggi/Documenti a curi di Filberto Menna, 7.)

A comprehensive, well illustrated work, covering the early years of the S.I. and divided into three major sections; 'L'Internazionale Situazionista', 'Documenti', and 'Cronologia, Schede bio-bibliografiche, Glossario, Bibliografia'. The documents section includes many key texts, some reproduced in facsimile (eg. part of Jorn's 'Peinture détournée' — 1959, and 'Ein Kultureller Putsch — wahrend Ihr schlaft!' — 1959). The 'bio-bibliographies' are of Constant, Guy Debord, Pinot-Gallizio, and Asger Jorn. There is also a general bibliography of much continental material (mostly Italian) not included in this bibliography. Also by Bandini; Urbanisme Unitare: la critica all'urbanistica e al funzionalismo teorizzata dall'Internazionale Situazionista. *Progettare In Più*. (Milan), (10), 1975. *Reference from Bandini, p. 385.

5.

Barrot, Jean. *What is situationism?: critique of the Situationist International*. London: Unpopular Books, 1987. 56 p., ill.

Pamphlet with cover of skulls with black text on yellow card. Latest edition published as; *What is Situationism?* Fort Bragg, CA.: Flatland, 1991. 52 p. First published as; Critique of the Situationist International. *Red-Eye*. (1), Fall, 1979. "This text was written as a chapter of a much longer work, as yet unpublished, which is essentially a critical history of revolutionary theory and ideology, beginning with the work of Marx." — L.M. (translator). Both editions contain an appendix by Karen Eliot [Stewart Home] entitled 'Basic Banalities' first published in *Smile*. (London) (8), 1985. Also in *Red-Eye*. (1), is Bruce Elwell's 'Disappearence of the family fortune'. Barrot cites "the only critique of the S.I. which has appeared up to the present"; *Supplement au no. 301 de la Nouvelle Gazette Rhénane*. Paris: [Distributed by] Éditions de l'Oubli, 1975. *Reference from Barrot, p. 30.

6.

Batchelor, David. A little Situationism. *Artscribe*. (66), Nov — Dec. 1987, pp. 51-4, ill.

Introduction to a special feature on the S.I. Includes an interview with Daniel Buren discussing his relationship to the S.I. and the May

'68 events. "If you remember some of the speeches and the slogans in '68 — all of a sudden there were a lot of people from different sides starting to be a little more critical about the art scene, starting to think more clearly about a supposedly free situation. And to my knowledge it was only the Situationists who had addressed that problem previously." — Buren, p. 52.

7.

Beard, Steve. Situationism. In: Godfrey, John, (ed.). *A decade of i-deas: the encyclopaedia of the '80s.* London: Penguin, 1990. ISBN 0140129529: pp. 195-197.

As a good example of 'mainstream' comment here is the full text. "What started out as a street-level guerilla gameshow directed against the 'society of the spectacle' in May '68 became a Malcolm McLaren media event in '77 and an ICA museum event by '89. Quite appropriate really, given that by the semiotic-smart '80s the Situationist Internationale's [sic] brand of cultural revolution was already a living fossil. A new kind of resistance was called for in a demystified decade which saw the S.I.'s patent on the manufacture of subversive spectacle trade-marked as the standard Factory tested new marketing tool. Scandal, shock and disruption were no longer used to wake the slumbering masses but to stimulate the jaded consumer — eg. ZTT's Frankie scam, Katharine Hamnett's Pershing T-shirt stunt. After all that, plain dumbness begins to look almost radical." — Beard, pp. 195-197.

8.

Bell, David. *Take that situation.* Birmingham: Urban Morphology Research Group, 1991. 3 p.

Discussion paper from the School of Geography, University of Birmingham, B1S 2TT. 1991. Short text with bibliography, also distributed as a 3 page photocopy on acetate. " [W]hat I am offering here is a reasonably comprehensive bibliography, divided up thematically. I hope that those commentators currently assessing festivals, theme parks and shopping malls around the globe will trace a few connections, even if they decide not to continue the revolution of everyday life." — Bell, p. 2. Contains references to; Bell, David. *Cities of the mind.* Birmingham: Urban Morphology Research Group Discussion Paper, 1991; and Hall, Tim. *The use of urban spectacle in the regeneration of blighted urban areas: some preliminary considerations*. Birmingham: Urban Morphology Research Group, 1991. For more on the S.I. and urbanism see; Bukatman, Scott. There's always tomorrowland: Disney and the hypercinematic experience. *October*. (57), Summer 1991, pp. 55-78, ill. ISBN 026275077. Includes chapter 'Situationist cities', pp. 63-66.; and Hatton, Brian. Tricky Situations. *Building Design*. (944), July 7, 1989, pp. 24-25., ill.

9.

Bell, David. *Situationists and the city: text for research seminar*. Birmingham: School of Geography, University of Birmingham, 1992. 9 p.

Abstract. "The Situationist International developed a set of techniques to explore the urban environment with the explicit aim of promoting a revolutionary critique of the existing society of the spectacle. By investigating the emotional contours of the city, they hoped ultimately to create an entirely new urban milieu in which citizens could engage in playful interaction in situations of their own construction. After describing the situationists' ideas for this new unitary urbanism, the paper goes on to examine a number of urban phenomena in the light of the situationist critique." Another article with an architectural slant; Miller, R. The Situationists, resurrecting the avant-garde. *Progressive Architecture*. 72 (9), 1991, p. 139-140.

10.

Berreby, Gerard, (ed.). *Documents relatifs à la fondation de l'Internationale situationniste: 1948-1957*. Paris: Éditions Allia, 1985. 651 p., ill. (some col.). ISBN 2904235051.

Massive anthology including many articles by Lettriste Internationale members; all Lettriste Internationale publications; Asger Jorn's *Pour la forme* (1958); and a colour facsimile of Jorn's and Debord's *Fin de Copenhagen* (1957). In Dutch, French, German, and Italian.

11.

Blazwick, Iwona, (ed.), in consultation with Mark Francis, Peter Wollen and Malcolm Imrie. *An endless adventure... an endless passion... an endless banquet: A situationist scrapbook*. London: I.C.A. and Verso, 1989. 96 p., ill. ISBN 0860919838.

With sandpaper covers. Contains three sections: 'The Situationist International: selected documents from 1957 to 1962', 'Documents:

4

the S.I. in Britain', and 'Fall out: a British inheritance, 1966-1988'. The first section merely reprints material from Knabb [35]. The second section includes: 'Psychogeographic maps of Venice', 1957 by Ralph Rumney, and 'Notice to contributors' (Sigma) by Alexander Trocchi, 1964. The third section includes: excerpts from *Heatwave* by Christopher Gray and Charles Radcliff, 'King Mob excerpts', 'Ramifications of situationist theory' from *Omphalos* 1970 by Paul Sieveking, 'The society of spectacle: an interview with Brigitte Bardot' from *Klepht*, 1968 by Ron Hunt and Chris MacConway, Malcolm McLaren's 'Oliver Twist' Sex Pistols manifesto, 1978, 'Orientation for the use of a context and the context for the use of an orientation', 1987 by Karen Eliot, and 'Narrative Architecture Today' from *Gamma City Special Issue*, 1985, by Nigel Coates. Other sandpaper covered publications include the album cover for *The Return of the Durutti Column*, Factory Records, 1979 and the exhibition catalogue entitled; *Daniel Moynihan: an exhibition at the Grob Gallery 20 Dering St, London W1; 13th May — 20th June 1992*. London: Grob Gallery, 1992. [12] p. This was printed in an edition of 2000 and consisted of the transcript of a conversation between the artist and Damien Hirst.

12.
Bonnett, Alastair. Situationism, geography and poststructuralism. *Environment and Planning D: Society and Space.* 7, 1989, pp. 131-146.

Abstract. "After an introduction to situationism and the theory of the spectacle, the movement's intellectual roots in postwar French Marxism are summarised. The situationist theory of social subversion and a contemporary example of the practice are then introduced. Situationism's critique of human geography and the development of similar perspectives within geography and other disciplines are assessed. It is suggested that situationism immobilises political judgment and that this tendency is paralleled within the poststructuralist philosophies of Derrida, Lyotard, and Baudrillard." — Bonnett. Includes a bibliography which includes two seemingly germane articles; Harvey, D. Flexible accumulation through urbanisation: reflections on 'post-modernism' in the American city. *Antipode* (19), 1987, pp. 260-286.; and Ley, D and Olds, K. Landscape as spectacle: world's fairs and the culture of the heroic consumption. *Environment and Planning D: Society and Space.* 6, 1988, pp. 191-212.

13.

Bonnett, Alastair. The Situationist legacy. *Variant*. (9), Autumn 1991, pp. 28-33, ill. ISSN 09548815.

Discussion of contemporary use and abuse of Situationist ideas. "I could conclude then by stating that a) the situationists have been depoliticized/postmodernized and b) they had it coming. This would be true enough but would miss what is the most exciting part of the situationist legacy. A part, moreover, that is generally side lined by the S.I.'s modern day interpreters. I am talking about the situationist critique of everyday space." — Bonnett, pp. 32.

14.

Bonnett, Alastair. Art, ideology, and everyday space: subversive tendencies from Dada to postmodernism. *Environment and Planning D: Society and Space*. 10, 1992, pp. 69-86, ill.

Abstract. "This is a paper about the transgression of the boundary between art and everyday space. It traces the development of a practical and theoretical critique of this divide from Dada and surrealism to situationism and postmodernism, whilst showing how these movements have themselves often perpetuated a specialized notion of cultural production. The ultimate failure of these movements, with the exception of situationism, to develop a coherent and effective challenge to the dualism art — everyday space is related to their reliance upon the artistic ideologies of anti-art, indifference, and spontaneism." — Bonnett, p. 69.

15.

Brown, Bill. The look we look at: T.J. Clark's walk back to the Situationist International. *Arts Magazine*. 63 (5), Jan. 1989, pp. 61-64.

This is a critique of T. J. Clark's *The painting of modern life* [18]. Bill Brown is also the editor of a Situationist journal, *Not Bored!* "The question that this article will take up is: Why does T.J. Clark's *The painting of modern life: Paris in the art of Manet and his followers* introduce the *name* of the Situationist International and the notion of 'the spectacle' into a discourse that was already 'situationist' even if Clark chose to call it 'the social history of art'?" — Brown, p. 61.

16.
Calluori, Raymond Anthony. *Cultural terrorism: British Punk and the unity of misery in everyday life.* (Subculture, Youth Rock).
Rutgers University N.Y. PHD. 1984: 133 p. *Reference OCLC.

Other relevant dissertations include:
Nehring, Neil Robert. *The destructive character: Walter Benjamin and a situationist approach to English literature and pop music since the 1930s.* University of Michigan, 1985. PH.D. 366 p. *Reference OCLC.
O'Conner, John Edward. *Revolution and the society of the spectacle: a critical analysis of selected plays by Howard Brenton.* University of Washington, PH.D. 1989. 249 p. *Reference OCLC.
Picher, Marie-Claire Antoinette. *Spectacle and power: towards a theory of postmodern avant-garde theater.* New York University. PH.D. 1989. 681 p. *Reference *Dissertation abstracts online.* "Source: Volume 50/09-A of *Dissertation abstracts international.* Page 2708. Order no: AAD90-04232".
Slawikowski, John Witold. *Situationist theory: the Situationist International and its supersession.* University of Illinois at Urbana-Champaign, 1976. PH.D. 399 p. *Reference from *Dissertation abstracts online.* "Source: Volume 37/05-A of *Dissertation abstracts international,* p. 3161. Order no. AAD76-24177".

17.
Carr, C. The Situationist situation: what we talk about when we talk about the avant-garde. *Voice Literary Supplement.* April, 1990, pp. 18-19, ill.

A review of three publications; Blazwick [11], Sussman [57], and Home [31], "It's still difficult at times to separate Situationist history from the attendant mythology: art history détourned. More famous now than they ever were during their 'brief moment in time', this group must still serve some function. Perhaps — as Debord says of movie stars — they are created 'by the need we have for them'. There are no avant-gardes anymore. They disappeared with modernism, into the museums." — Carr, p. 19.

18.
Clark, Timothy James, [1943-]. *The painting of modern life: Paris in the art of Manet and his followers.* London: Thames and Hudson, 1990. xv, 338 p., ill. ISBN 0500275750 pbk.

"The notion of spectacle ... was designed first and foremost as a weapon of combat, and contains within itself a more or less bitter (more or less resigned) prediction of its own reappearance in some such form as this, between the covers of a book on art. Although I shall not wrestle in the toils of this contradiction too long, I wish at least to alert the reader to the absurdity involved in making 'spectacle' part of the canon of academic Marxism. If once or twice in the text my use of the word carries a faint whiff of Debord's chiliastic serenity I shall be satisfied." Clark, p. 10. Originally published; New York: Knopf, 1984, and first published by Thames & Hudson, 1985. T. J. Clark was a member of the short-lived English section of the S.I. up to December 1967 and was also a part of the 'Heatwave' group.

19.
Crary, Jonathan. Spectacle, attention, counter-memory. *October.* (50), Fall 1989, pp. 97-107, ill. ISBN. 026275200X.

"This paper was originally presented at the Sixth International Colloquium on Twentieth Century French Studies, Revolutions 1889-1989, at Columbia University, March 30 — April 1, 1989." Examines the term 'spectacle' and the history of its usage in the work of Lefebvre, Debord, and T.J. Clark. Also by Crary; Eclipse of the spectacle. In : Wallis, B, (ed.). *Art after modernism: rethinking representation.* New York; Boston: New Museum of Contemporary Art; D. R. Godine, 1984: pp. 283-294.

20.
Crawford, Margeret. The Hacienda must be built. *Design Book Review.* (24), 1992, pp. 38-42, ill.

A review of four S.I. related books Marcus [42], Blazwick [11], Debord [91], and Knabb [35]. She suggests the current interest in the situationists abounds because their; "self-consciousness about discursive practices, their use of fragments to disrupt and break down dominant narratives, and intentional blurring between high and low and abstraction and representation prefigure many postmodern concerns." — Crawford, p. 39.

21.
Davidson, Steef. *The Penguin book of political comics.* Harmondsworth: Penguin, 1982. 205 p., ill. ISBN 0140060359.

Translated by Hester and Marianne Velmans. First published as; *Beeldenstorm: de ontwikkeling van de politieke strip (1965-75).* Amsterdam:

Van Gennep, 1978. 176 p., ill. ISBN 9060123158. Davidson was a member of Provo and editor of the Dutch underground magazine *Om*. Of particular interest is the chapters 'The return of the Durutti Column', 'The international conspiracy' and 'Paris May '68'.

22.
Dumontier, Pascal. *Les situationnistes et Mai 68: théorie et pratique de la révolution (1966-1972)*. Paris: Éditions Gérard Lebovici, 1990. 307 p. ISBN 2851842269.

An in-depth look at the S.I. during a period that is dominated by the May 68 events and the break up of the movement. The research drew heavily on the archives of the Bibliothèque de Documentation Internationale Contemporaine (Nanterre) and l'Institute International d'Histoire Sociale (Amsterdam). It includes an extensive bibliography (pp. 226-239) of relevant French language material and an English translation of 'Report from the delegates conference held in Wolsfeld and Trier, January 17th-19th, 1970.' Text chiefly in French. The references include; Buck, Guillaume. *Approche théorique de l'Internationale situationniste (1957-1971) et ses rapports avec la théorie et le mouvement anarchiste.* Paris: Mémoire de maîtrise de sciences politiques, sous la direction de S. Picard, 1987. 60 p.

23.
Dunbar, David. The picturesque ruins of the Situationist International. *Performance.* (58), Summer 1989, pp. 30-43, ill.

Ostensibly an article about the relationship between the S.I. and performance art and how this relationship is based on; "a confused mixture of the radical reputation of the S.I. with the mistaken belief that they were political artists interested in revolutionary 'happenings'." — Dunbar, p. 42. Also examines the S.I. history and Debord's theories of anti-art.

24.
Francis, Mark. It's all over: the material (and anti-material) evidence. In: Sussman [57] pp. 16-19, ill.

A short explanation of the organization of the exhibition, how it was divided into (1) détournement (2) dérive and psychogeography (3) pittura industriale (4) unitary urbanism and (5) tracts and posters produced by the Council for the Maintenance of the Occupations at the Sorbonne in May 1968. He also mentions the so called 'fall out' period which problematically included artists such as Art & Language and Daniel Buren. "Two aspects of the discovery of these notes [by Guy Debord, dated 10 March 1961 and deposited in the Silkeborg Museum, Denmark] seem apposite to any remarks about the intentions and purposes of an exhibition such as this. The first is the very existence of this archive in the 'public domain' and the fact that it is clearly intended for research purposes; the second is its clear and even dialectical method of organization ... It lent credence to our supposition that putting together and presenting the collection of models, films, tracts, art works, books, and leaflets that were issued in the name of the S.I. or that specifically used the strategies they developed ... could and should be attempted." — Francis, p.16.

25.

Gombin, Richard. *The origins of modern leftism*. London: Pelican, 1975. 144 p. ISBN 0140218467.

Translated by Michael K. Perl from; *Les origines du gauchisme*. Paris: Éditions du Seuil, 1971. See especially chapter 3, 'A critique of everyday life', and 4 'The theory of council communism', pp. 57-117. "The influence of H. Lefebvre is undeniable (and reciprocal), but that of the dadaists, the surrealists, the lettrists and other *avant-garde* groups was also apparent. This current, cultural in origin, was to take up the Marxist critique once more, in particular that portion of Marx that was Hegelian in origin, as interpreted by Lukàcs." — Gombin, p. 61. See also his; The ideology and practice of contestation seen through recent events in France. In : Apter, David E. and Joll, James. *Anarchism today*. London: Macmillan, 1971. ISBN 333120418: pp. 14-33.

26.

Gray, Christopher, (ed.). *Leaving the Twentieth Century: the incomplete work of the Situationist International*. London: Free Fall Publications, 1974. 167 p., ill. ISBN 0950353205.

Translations of articles published originally in *Internationale situationniste* [33]. With additional introductory texts and a conclusion. "Their quest was for the perfect formula, the magic charm that would disperse the evil spell. This pursuit of the perfect intellectual formula meant inevitably that situationist groups were based on a hierarchy of intellectual ability — and thus on disciples and followers, on fears and exhibitionism, the whole political horror trip. After their initial period, creativity, apart from its intellectual forms, was denied expression — and in this lies the basic instability and sterility of their own organisation." —Gray, pp. 166-167. "Members of the Surburban Press and the Wicked Messengers were involved in the printing and typesetting, and Jamie Reid did the graphics for the book." — Savage, in Reid [301], p. 40. The same source states that it was originally published in an edition of 4000. Letters in the 'Alexander Trocchi Archive' indicate that the book was ready for the printers in 1972 and that Trocchi was to write a preface. This archive also contains a 18 page typescript of Gray's commentary in the anthology written in either 1972 or 1973. The book was reviewed by; Berger, John. Lost prophets. *New Society*. 6/3/75, pp. 600-601. Berger describes the S.I. as; "one of the most lucid and pure political formulations of the 1960s."

27.

Harper, Clifford. *Anarchy: a graphic guide.* London: Camden Press, 1987. 196 p., ill. ISBN 0948491221.

Includes a summary account of the influence of the S.I. on the sixties counter-cultural scene including the Provos, Watts, the Beats, Berkeley, the Diggers, Strasbourg, and May '68. Unfortunately there is no attempt at a portrait of Debord in the style of Frans Masereel, but as the title suggests there are some stunning illustrations included in this 'beginners guide' to Anarchism. "Creative subjectivity is in essence revolutionary because in its attempts to fulfil its aims it must come up against the bounds of this repressive society. In order to succeed in its aims it must break through any restraints." — Harper, p. 149. The Situationists are also covered in the latest massive history of anarchism. Marshall, Peter. *Demanding the impossible: a history of anarchism.* London: Fontana, 1993. 767 p. ISBN 0006862454 (pbk). See especially pp. 549-553.

28.

Henri, Adrian. *Environments and Happenings.* London: Thames and Hudson, 1974. 216 p., ill. ISBN 0500181438 pbk.

Brief mention of the S.I. but describes the ferment of art actions that the S.I. have, in some quarters, become associated with. These include the Motherfuckers, Black Mask, Fluxus and Provo.

29.

Heynen, Hilde. Architecture under the regime of the Spectacle. *Forum International*. 3 (14), 1992, pp. 50-55, ill.

"Hilde Heynen is an architecture theorist. She teaches at the Katholieke Universiteit Leuven." — *Forum International* editorial comment. Further discussion of the S.I., the spectacle, Debord and architecture.

30.

Hewison, Robert. *Future tense: a new art for the nineties*. London: Methuen, 1990. 190 p., ill. ISBN 0413634302.

Not a particularly enlightening use of S.I. themes, see especially preface 'A parable' — pp. 23-31. "A specific event in London in June 1989 [exhibition I.C.A.] struck me as having particular ironies for anyone interested in the future of what used to be called the avant-garde." — Hewison, p. 23. Also includes a section on Nigel Coates and Narrative Architecture Today (NATO).

31.

Home, Stewart. *The assault on culture: utopian currents from Lettrisme to Class War*. London: Aporia Press and Unpopular Books, 1988. 115 p. ISBN 094851888X.

2nd edition published by AK Press, Stirling, 1991. [128]p. ISBN 1873176309. A ground-breaking reference work on this century's little known avant-garde art movements. It gives brief but informative histories of such movements as Cobra, the S.I., Fluxus and Mail Art. Includes a selected bibliography that charts the often obscure samizdat publications describing the activities of these and other groups. The author writes from "a position of engagement" and this is reflected in the polemical tone employed. The avant-garde is notorious for its obfuscation of its own history and Home's version of events has caused some controversy in the milieu. Home offers this critique of Vaneigem's non-materialist notion of art; "If art, from a materialist perspective, is a process which occurs in bourgeois society, there can be no question of its *realisation*. Such an idea is mystical since it implies not only that art has an essence, but that as a category it is autonomous of social structures. To undertake its *realisation* and *suppression* is an attempt to *save* this mental set at the very moment the category is *abolished*. Art disappears from the museums *only* to reappear *everywhere!* So much for the *autonomous* practice of the *proletariat*, this is actually the old bourgeois dream of a *universal* category which will propagandise for social cohesion." Home, p. 43. For short reviews of the book see; Anon. Plagiarism/the assault on culture. *Artists Newsletter.* Nov. 1988; Ford, Simon. The assault on culture. *ARLIS News-sheet.* (96) May/June 1992, p. 8; and North, Richard. Ghoul Daze. *New Musical Express.* 20/8/1988. See also [319-331]. In the introduction to a Polish edition of the book (to be published in 1993 by Wydawnictwo Hotel Sztuki, Warszawa) Home makes much of the connections between the S.I., the far right, and occult societies. He also reviews developments in utopian currents since the book was written in 1987 including the historification of Fluxus, the 1989 S.I. exhibition, and the growing significance of Neoism.

32.

International situationniste. *Débat d'orientation de l'ex-Internationale situationniste.* Paris: Centre de recherche sur la question sociale, 1974. 80 p.

Internal documents, 1969-1971, debating possible strategies for the group post-May '68. "Reprints of documents published between 26 August 1969 and 28 January 1971; chiefly in French, with two documents in English." — *Reference OCLC.

33.

Internationale situationniste 1958-1969. Paris: Éditions Champ Libre, 1975. [c. 600 p.], ill. ISBN 2851840363.

Complete facsimile edition of the journal nos. 1-12 (June 1958—Sept. 1969). "The review ... was published for eleven years (and moreover during this time it managed to bankrupt its two successive printers). It dominated this period, and it attained its goal. It was very important for passing on our theses in this epoch." Debord and Sanguinetti [84], p. 90. It was first published in one volume by; Amsterdam: Van Gennep, 1970. First German edition published in two volumes including the original layout and illustrations as; *Situationistische Internationale 1958-1969.* Hamburg: Nautilus, 1977. An anonymous and brief review of the 1970 edition appeared in the *Times Literary Supplement.* (3598), 19.2.71, p. 205, under the heading 'Sectacular'. "What is interesting is that there is so little change over the decade: the same names reappear, the same ideas recur, the same squabbles erupt. What change there is derives from the outside world: the imperialist war shifts from Algeria to Vietnam, the political use of pin-ups shifts from bikinis to nudes, the growth of the student rebellion increases editorial self-confidence." — Anon, p. 205. A Spanish edition of selected texts was published as; Subirats, Eduardo, (ed. and trans.). *Textos situacionistas: Crítica de la vida cotidiana.* Barcelona: Anagrama, 1973. 109 p. (Documentos). (Cuadernos Anagrama, 55). *Reference from Hansen [114], p. 152. Also from Spain; *Textos situacionistas sobre los Consejos Obreros.* Madrid: Campo Abierto Ediciones, 1977. 120 p., ill. ISBN 8474460026. (Debate libertario; 2. Serie: Acción directa). Translated by Juan Fonseca; and *Panfletos y escritos de la Internacional Situacionista.* Madrid: Editorial Fundamentos, 1976. 108 p. (Cuadernos pràcticos; no. 26) An article from the journal translated by José Domínguez Tenreiro. Title on cover 'Crear por fin la situació que haga imposible la marcha atràs'. *References from OCLC. An Italian translation of (1-2) published as; *Internazionale situazionista.* Genova: E.C.A.T. Libri, 1975. Vol. 1. (79 p.). *Reference from Hansen [114], p. 157. Also selected texts published by; Ghirardi, Sergio and Varini, Dario. *Internazionale situazionista (ce n'a été qu'un debut).* Milano: La Salamandra, 1976. 298 p. (Filo rosso, 5). *Reference from Hansen [114], p. 158.

34.
Kaplan, Alice and Ross, Kristin, (eds). Introduction [Everyday life special issue]. *Yale French Studies.* (73), 1987, pp.1-4.
"To advance a theory of everyday life is to elevate lived experience to the status of a critical concept — not merely in order to describe lived experience, but in order to change it ... In France the dazzling technical innovations of structuralism were produced during the same decades that saw an intense intellectual and political critique — both inside and outside academic institutions — of consumer society. This questioning was to culminate in the events surrounding May '68." — Kaplan and Ross, p. 1. Also by Ross, with some mention of the S.I., see; Ross, K. *The emergence of social space: Rimbaud and the Paris Commune.* London: Macmillan, 1988. *Reference from Bonnett [14], p. 85.

35.
Knabb, Ken, (ed.). *Situationist International anthology.* Berkeley: Bureau of Public Secrets, 1981. x, 406 p. ISBN 0939682001.
English translations by Ken Knabb (in collaboration with Nadine Bloch and Joël Cornuault) of selected articles from the journal

Internationale situationniste [33] and other sources. "The most comprehensive collection of texts from the group that made the most comprehensive, lucid and adventurous assault on modern society. Film scripts and articles on psychogeography and the creation of situations; critiques of art, urbanism and everyday life; analyses of the global society of the spectacle; documents from the May 1968 revolt in France (which the Situationists' new tactics contributed toward provoking)." — Knabb, publicity material. Recently published from the *Situationist International anthology* in a new translation is; *Watts 1965: the decline and fall of the spectacle-commodity economy.* Berkeley: Bureau of Public secrets, July 1992. 4 p. Disseminated as comment on the LA riots of 1992.

36.
Kumar, Krishan. Situationism. In : Bullock, Allan, Oliver Stallybrass and Stephen Trombley. *The Fontana dictionary of modern thought.* London: Fontana Press, 1988. New & revised edition. ISBN 0006861296: p. 779.

A short entry illustrating the difficulty some academics have with the S.I. "The radical philosophy of a group of mainly French social and cultural critics whose views first appeared in an avant-garde magazine *Internationale situationniste* [33], from 1958 onwards ... Instead of the take-over of the state and economy that was the aim of most revolutionaries, they demanded a 'revolution of everyday life' that would transform personal relationships and cultural outlooks." — Kumar.

37.
Lefebvre, Henri. The everyday and everydayness. *Yale French Studies.* (73), 1987, pp. 7-11.

"Today we see a worldwide tendency to uniformity. Rationality dominates, accompanied but not diversified by irrationality; signs, rational in their way, are attached to things in order to convey the prestige of their possessors and their place in the hierarchy." — Lefebvre, p. 7. A short overview by Lefebvre of his conception of the everyday. Also by Lefebvre; *The critique of everyday life.* London: Verso, 1991.

38.

Maayan, Myriam D. From aesthetic to political vanguard: the Situationist International, 1957-1968. *Arts Magazine*. 63 (5), Jan. 1989, pp. 49-53, ill.

A straight-forward account of the development of the S.I. from its artistic beginnings to its later, supposed, repudiation of art. "This article is an expanded version of a paper that I delivered to the 14th annual meeting of the Western Society for French History and which was reproduced in that Society's *Proceedings*, 14 (1987)."

39.

Maragliano, Giorgio. The invisible insurrection: the Situationists revisited — détournement rendered autonomous and removed from its context of subversion. *Flash Art*. (147), Summer 1989, pp. 87-90, ill.

"Since the absolute and amnesiac present of the mass media (the phrase is Debord's) can live up to itself and its own dominion only by regular scansions of reasonably reactivating and then once again expunging the memory of the past, there is some point in making haste (before the curtain drops) if we want to ask ourselves what the Situationist International was all about, and thus to track its influence, both secret and manifest, on phenomena as various as Malcolm McLaren and the *Great Rock and Roll Swindle*, 'allegorical procedures', 'commodity art', Jean Baudrillard, et alia." — Maragliano, p. 87.

40.

Marcus, Greil. How extreme was it? The long walk of the Situationist International. *Voice Literary Supplement*. (7), May 1982, pp. 13-19.

An enthusiastic, substantial, review of Knabb [35] which had a noteworthy influence on the introduction of the Situationists to mainstream America. "The situationist program — as opposed to the situationist project, situationist practice — came down to Lautréamont and workers' councils... These were the situationist touchstones — and, oddly, they were left unexamined." — Marcus, p. 18. He also comments on the aesthetics of the original journal [33]. "Wonderfully illustrated with photos, comics, reproductions of advertisements, drawings, and maps, *Internationale situationniste* had an elegant, straight-forward design: flat, cool, and direct. It made a simple point: what we have written is meant seriously and should be read seriously." —Marcus, p. 19. Supplement came with *The Village Voice*. XXVII (19), May 11, 1982.

41.

Marcus, Greil. The cowboy philospher. *Artforum*. March 1986, pp. 85-91, ill.
Could be seen as the seminal work of the Situationist's entry into the
mainstream art world press. The cowboy philosopher comes from
the comic strip *Le Retour de la Colonne Durrutti* by André Bertrand,
1966. Marcus follows the cowboy's 'dérive' from Michèle Bernstein,
through May '68 to his appearance on a Mekons record sleeve in
1985. A slightly different version published in; *Chemical Imbalance*.
(USA), 2 (2), [1989], pp. 42-48, ill.

42.

Marcus, Greil. *Lipstick traces: a secret history of the twentieth century*.
London: Secker & Warburg, 1989. 496 p., ill. ISBN 0436273381.
A difficult book to summarize due to its unconventional structure
and its wide-ranging historical references. There are some interesting
pieces of information here but they are hard to pin down and difficult
to relocate. "This is no mere search for cultural antecedents. Instead,
what Marcus so brilliantly shows is that various kinds of angry,
intransigent and absolute demands — on society, art, and all
governing structures of everyday life — seem to be coded in phrases,
images, and actions passed on invisibly by people who have never
heard of each other." — Blurb inside front cover. See also [332-339].

43.

Martos, Jean-François. *Histoire de l'Internationale situationniste*. Paris:
Éditions Gérard Lebovici, 1989. 281 p. ISBN 285184217X.
A straight forward 'official' history of the S.I. told through its
publications. It also includes a useful table of contents that in note
form lists the significant events of 1952-1972. The book is divided into
the chapters 'Ab origine (1952-1957)', 'Ars longa, vita brevis (1958-
1961)', 'Urbi et orbi (1962-1967)', 'Dies irae (Mai 1968)', 'Ne varietur
(1970-1972)'. Text in French.

44.

Miller, John. The consumption of everyday life. *Artscribe*. (67), Jan-Feb
1988, pp. 46-52, ill.
Discussion around the artists and writers Haim Steinbach, Baudelaire,
Duchamp, Michael Fried, and Walter Benjamin's *flâneur*. An example
of the function of Situationist concepts in 'critical' discourse.

"Steinbach's art consists *solely* of putting things on pedestals. Alone, this might constitute a refined form of idolatry, but it is performed without the requistite fervour. By profaning the secular, Steinbach lays bare the phantasm which Guy Debord calls the spectacle. By targeting the commodity he 'obviates' the pre-eminent configuration of all possible objects because only in universality does the commodity fulfil its logical potential." — Miller, p. 48.

45.
Ohrt, Roberto. *Phantom Avantgarde: eine Geschichte der Situationistischen International und der modernen Kunst.* Hamburg: Nautilus; Galerie van de Loo, 1990. 333 p., ill. (some col.) ISBN 3894011688.
A revision of the author's doctoral thesis (Universität Hamburg, 1989), which was originally presented under the title; *Kunst, Situation, Aktion.* A substantial work with excellent illustrations. This item also includes a 'Biblio-Geographie', pp. 312-326, with much foreign language material not listed in this bibliography. See also; Sanders, R.J. *Beweging tegen de schijn: de situationisten, een avant-garde.* Amsterdam: Huis aan de Drie Grachten, 1989. 320 p., ill. ISBN 9063881428; Perniola, Mario. I situationisti. *Agaragar.* (4) Rome 1972.; Marelli, G.F. *Internationale situationniste, theoria come practica.* Universitat Mailand, 1983.; Prem, Heimrad. *Bilder 1959-1965, Dokumentation und Lagerkatalog III.* München, 1974.; Zimmer, H.P. *H.P. Zimmer: Bilder, Objekte Räume.* München: Kunstverein Wolfsburg, 1986. 256 p., ill.; *Uwe Lausen: Bilder, Zeichnungen, Texte, 1960-1970: 11. Juli bis 19 August 1984.* München: Stätische Galerie in Lenbachhaus, 1984; Tacussel, Patrick. *L'attraction sociale le dynamisme de l'imaginaire dans la société monocéphale.* Paris: Libr. des Méridiens, 1984. 204 p. ISBN 2865630919; and Kiwitz, Peter. *Lebenswelt und Lebenskunst: Perspektiven einer kritischen Theorie des sozialen Lebens.* München: W. Fink, 1986. 230 p. ISBN 3770523229. See also a 'pro-situ' manifesto published by Nautilus; Subrealistic Movement. *Vacation of Hegel: latest campaigns of critico-practical theory.* Hamburg: Nautilus, 1979, 12 p. "This text, published in english, french and russian, is an extract of "Jetzt!" a subrealistic manifesto, which came out in October 1979 in West-Germany." — Inside front cover. "We hold the feeble, the compromising in contempt, because the storm is imminent which will obliterate this oppressive atmosphere. The mass-uprising of this epoch stands ready on the horizon to turn the tide of history itself." — Back cover.

46.

Plant, Sadie. The Situationist International: a case of spectacular neglect. *Radical Philosophy*. (55), Summer 1990, pp. 3-10.

"The following discussion goes some way towards correcting this neglect with an indication of the relevance of Situationist ideas to contemporary political and philosophical debate and a consideration of the historical and intellectual contexts in which the Situationists worked." — Plant, p. 3. The article also discusses the role of recuperation and recent 'critical developments' such as *Variant, Here and Now, Vague* and *Smile*.

47.

Plant, Sadie. *The most radical gesture: the Situationist International in a postmodern age*. London: Routledge, 1992. 226 p. ISBN 0415062225.

Sadie Plant does a thorough job unravelling how the S.I. influences, precurses and provides critical positions in relation to postmodernist discourse (particularly that surrounding Jean Baudrillard and Jean-François Lyotard). *The most radical gesture* also explores the S.I.'s influence on May '68, Punk and recent manifestations of related interest such as the Festival of Plagiarism. Reviews; Moore, Suzanne. The politics of having a good time. *The Guardian*. Thursday May 28 1992, [p. 31]. "*The most radical gesture* lucidly reminds us of the passion of a politics that was actually passionate about living, where out on the street one can be touched by what André Breton called 'the breath of the possible'. And though the post-modernist may fiddle while cities burn, the street remains more than a metaphor." — Moore. A short review but reproduces a letter signed by Bernstein, Debord, and Wolman (13 October 1955) concerning the demolition of the Chinese quarter in London; Walter, Natasha. Angry at the corpse in their mouths. *The Independent*. Saturday 13 June 1992. Weekend section, [p. 32]. A brief, critical review of *The most radical gesture* complaining that "Plant's very turgid, very academic style does little to communicate the revolutionary fervour or even the pure fun of the Situationists ... grinding their ideas to dust in the service of cultural studies." — Walter; and Young, Elizabeth. Born modern. *New Statesman and Society*. 8 May 1992, [p. 47]. A half-page and more positive account of the book. "An analysis of Situationism is long overdue, and Sadie Plant's rigorous account finally gives it credit for its enormous contribution to postwar theory and revolutionary politics. The Situationists had immense insight and a real capacity to rouse people to action from within the numbing blandishments of the hyperreal." — Young. See also: Marcus, Greil. You could catch it. *London Review of Books.* 25 March 1993, pp 12-13; Chase, Bob. Serious matters in a playful age. *Times Higher Education Supplement.* April 9, 1993, p.22.

48.
Raspaud, Jean-Jacques and Jean-Pierre Voyer (de l'Institut de Préhistoire Contemporaine, B.P. 20-05, Paris.). *L'Internationale situationniste: chronologie, bibliographie, protagonistes (avec un index des noms insultés).* Paris: Éditions Champ Libre, 1972. 168 p.

A publication that forms a substantial index to the twelve issue of *Internationale situationniste* [33]. Contents include a table of S.I. members, an index of S.I. members cited in the journal, 'index des noms cités ou insultés', 'table des ouvrages cités', a bibliography of works by the S.I. and on the S.I., a reproduction of the contents pages of the journal and a list of S.I. members and their publications and articles. Also by Jean-Pierre Voyer; *Une enquête sur la nature et les causes de la misère des gens.* Paris: Éditions Champ Libre, 1976. 120 p. ISBN 2851840533 ; *Rapport sur l'état des illusions dans notre parti, (suivi de) Révélations sur le principe du monde.* Paris: Institut de préhistoire contemporaine, 1979. 183 p.; *Lettre ouverte aux citoyens du F.H.A.R.* Tract de l'Institut de Préhistoire Contemporaine, Paris, 10 novembre 1971. *Reference from Dumontier [22], p. 230; *Hécatombe.* Paris: La Nuit, 1991. 353 p., ill. ISBN 2909059006. His collected correspondence.; and *Introduction à la science de la publicité.* Paris: Éditions Champ Libre, 1975. 91 p., ill. ISBN 2851840304.

49.
Roberts, John. Eleven theses on the Situationist International. In: Roberts, John. *Selected errors: writings on art and politics 1981-90.* London: Pluto Press, 1992. ISBN 0745304974: pp. 114-125.

The eleven theses in question are entitled, the revolutionary party, the society of the spectacle, a critique of the everyday, unitary urbanism, desire, the carnivalesque/festivity, popular art/high culture, détournement, dérive, the potlatch, and the avant-garde. The text seems to have been written around the time of the 1989 exhibition although this is the first time it has been published.

Roberts believes that "secreted at the very heart of the S.I.'s proletarianism is a romantic anti-capitalism; which is why in many ways its cultural slogans, rather than other aspects of the group's work, have remained so enduring for so many people on the left over the years." — Roberts, p. 119.

50.
Rohan, Marc. Paris '68: graffiti, posters, newspapers and poems of the events of May 1968. London: Impact Books, 1988. 142 p., ill. ISBN 0245547223.

Reproduces the front pages of the newspaper *Action* produced by the Comités d'Action. No specific mention of the Situationists or the Enragés but supplies countless examples of Situationist inspired slogans and graffiti. Also reproduces many of the simple but effective posters of the period (including the poster 'Young people too often worried about their future' a precursor of the punk safety-pin theme).

51.
Romild, Laura and Vincent, Jacques. *Échecs situationnistes*. Paris: Imprimerie de Copédith, 1988. 36 p.

*Reference and review from *Here and Now*. (7/8), p. 34. "A critique of the situationist project in theory and as practiced in the years following the dissolution of the Situationist International. The authors criticize a milieu turned in on itself, which used the funds available to it (through the publishing house Éditions Champ Libre) only to reproduce, celebrate and mythologise its own past, and advertise the intransigence of its own lifestyle, 'equivalent in culture and mentality to a kind of Albania.'" Romild and Vincent also attempt to destroy more Situationist myths; "The central point of the situationist myth is the famous appeal, for the general occupation strike and the formation of the workers' councils, published by the first Sorbonne Occupation Committee, with situationist participation, on 16th May 1968. That appeal, coming after the start of the strikes, had no effect, positive or negative, on the flow of events, and, in concrete terms, the situationists 'historic' activity stopped there." —From an unpublished translation.

52.
Section italienne de l'Internationale situationniste. *Écrits complets (1969-1972)*. Paris: Contre-Moule, 1988. 144 p.

Translated into French by Joël Gayraud and Luc Mercier. *Reference from Dumontier [22], p. 228. See also; Agamben, Giorgio ... [et al.] *I Situazionisti*. Roma: Manifestolibri, 1991. 94 p. ISBN 8872850010 (La Talpa di biblioteca; 1). *Reference from OCLC.

53.
Shipway, Mark. Situationism. In : Rubel, Maximilien and Crump, John (eds). *Non-market socialism in the nineteenth and twentieth centuries*. London: Macmillan Press, 1987. ISBN 0333413008: pp. 151-172.

"Situationism shared three main strengths in common with the other currents which represent non-market socialism. First the situationists recognised capitalism as a worldwide system embracing every existing nation-state ... Second, the situationists had a clear conception of what the establishment of a new non-market society would have to involve in terms of abolishing the essential characteristics of capitalism ... Third, the situationists believed that no other force in society could carry out the communist revolution apart from the working class." — Shipway, p. 165.

54.
Situationist International. *On the poverty of student life considered in its economic, political, psychological, sexual, and particularly intellectual aspects, and a modest proposal for its remedy*. Detroit: Black and Red, 1973. 24 p.

Cover title 'Ten days that shook the university' printed on yellow card, contents printed on blue paper. One of many English translations of *De la misère en milieu étudiant, considérée sous ses aspects économique, politique, psychologique, sexuel et notamment intellectuel et de quelques moyens pour y remédier*. [Paris]: Association fédérative générale des étudiants de Strasbourg, 1966. Reprinted; Paris: Éditions Champ Libre, 1976. 59 p. ISBN 2851840649. The first English translation was published in London in 1967. "This edition was translated by Donald Nicholson-Smith and T.J. Clark and was edited by Christopher Gray. The cover design offers a translation of the Strasbourg student, Andre Bertrand's, 'La Retour de la Colonne Durutti.'" Wilson, Andrew. *Documents of the avant-garde 1945-1990: catalogue 13*. London: Sam Fogg, 1991, p.7.

55.
Situationist International. *On the poverty of student life considered in its economic, political, psychological, sexual, and particularly intellectual aspects, and a modest proposal for its remedy.* London: Dark Star and Rebel Press, 1985. 33 p.

The first French version was published in 1966. This version includes the postscript 'If you make a social revolution, do it for fun', said to be "taken from the English language translation published by Éditions Champ Libre in 1972. [94 p., ill. (Bibliothèque asiatique; 10) in Chinese, French and English]" — t.p. verso. This short pamphlet is probably the most famous and widely available text by the Situationists. It has been reproduced in countless editions and has also been translated into many languages. The first edition in 1966 was published and printed by the students at Strasbourg (using the total student union fund for that year) with the help of the Situationist Mustapha Khayati and handed out on the first day of the new academic year. The event caused a scandal and can be seen to as a precursor to the student unrest that culminated in May '68. German translation by Pierre Gallissaires as; *Über das Elend im Studentenmilieu...* Hamburg: L. Schulenburg, 1977. 64 p., ill. *Reference from OCLC.

56.
Stansill, Peter and David Zane Mairowitz. *BAMN: outlaw manifestos and ephemera, 1965-1970.* Harmondsworth: Penguin, 1971. 280 p., ill. ISBN 0140032673.

Although this was published before 1972 it has been included because it is an essential collection of ephemeral material concerning the underground milieu of the late sixties. "This anthology covers many of the radical and visionary movements, groups, and cells of protest and propaganda of the past five years. It takes in the 'Provos' of Amsterdam, the Black Panthers, the Yippies, and the English Situationists, the Woman's Liberation Movement, the world-wide commune movement and the growing protest against ecological destruction." — Back cover. For more information on Provo, Kommune 1 and the Kabouters see; Duijn, Roel van. *Message of a wise Kabouter.* London: Duckworth, 1972. 98 p. ISBN 0715606115; Berke, Joseph, (ed.). *Counter culture.* London: Peter Owen, 1969. 405 p., ill. ISBN 720614031; and de Jong, Rudolf. Provos and Kabouters. In :

Apter, David E. and Joll, James. *Anarchism today*. London: Macmillan, 1971. ISBN 333120418: pp. 164-180. Also on Provo see; Vassart, Christian and Racine, Aimée. *Provos et provotariat: Un an de recherche participante en milieu provo*. Bruxelles: C.E.D.J., 1968. 160 p., ill. (Centre d'étude de la délinquance juvénile. Publication: no. 21). *Reference from OCLC. The group also produced a journal *Provo*. "The contributers to this landmark journal (June 1965-April 1967, 15 issues and 1 extra bulletin) form a roll-call of the Amsterdam underground happening movement whose activism and aspirations—an anarchist strain of Situationist thinking revealed by Constant's links with Provo (No.4 and 9)—are duly catalogued within it. The Provo group started by Robert Jasper Grootveld in 1965, became the model in Europe (and America, see No. 12 and 15) for this type of underground activity. In 1966 before the Destruction in Art Symposium a group of them visited London following an invitation from Gustav Metzger (No. 12). Their most poignant symbol became the White Bicycle of Amsterdam (No. 9) 'If you need one, find one, and when you don't need it leave it. Someone else will take it' (Rob Stolk). They termed their plans as 'White', a word which held a meaning similar to the 'Free' of the San Francisco Diggers." Wilson, Andrew. *Documents of the avant-garde 1945-1990: catalogue 13*. London: Sam Fogg, 1991, p.8.

57.
Sussman, Elisabeth, (ed.). *On the passage of a few people through a rather brief moment in time: the Situationist International 1957-1972*. Boston, Mass.: M.I.T. Press; Institute of Contemporary Art, Boston, 1989. vii, 200 p., ill. ISBN 0262231468.

Contents: 'Preface' by David A. Ross, 'Introduction' by Elisabeth Sussman [58], 'It's all over: the material (and anti-material) evidence' by Mark Francis [24], 'Bitter victory: the art and politics of the Situationist International' by Peter Wollen [62], 'Asger Jorn and the Situationist International' by Troels Andersen [105], 'An enormous and unknown chemical reaction: the experimental laboratory in Alba' by Mirella Bandini [123], 'Dismantling the spectacle: the cinema of Guy Debord' by Thomas Y Levin [100], 'Guy Debord's Mémoires: a Situationist Primer' by Greil Marcus [101], 'A selection of Situationist writing: imaginary maps of the real world', 'Situationist data', 'Checklist of the exhibition', and 'definitions'. The most obvious attempt at a recuperation of the S.I. has to be this 1989 travelling retrospective.

The show settled uncomfortably between two camps. One that saw it as an installation conceived in the spirit of the S.I. and the other which saw it as an historical retrospective, a survey show. However there was not enough contextualization for it to be a didactic show and their was not enough coherence in and between the work for it to be an installation. The show in its different manifestations in each country also revealed the nationalistic interests specific to each country. The exclusion of any precursors was also misleading although very much in the spirit of the S.I. itself.

58.
Sussman, Elisabeth. Introduction. In: Sussman, Elisabeth, (ed.). *On the passage of a few people through a rather brief moment in time: the Situationist International 1957-1972*. Boston, Mass.: M.I.T. Press; Institute of Contemporary Art, Boston, 1989, pp. 2-15, ill.
Recounts how the exhibition came about, with a very brief summary of Situationist concepts. Also discusses the problem of the post-1962 Situationist relationship to material objects and the exhibition. "After 1962, Guy Debord and those around him actively refused and negated the concept of art as a separate, exhibitable enterprise ... we have chosen to convey the broader historic cultural impact of the Situationists through the inclusion of statements from primary sources, the striking graphics of the journal, the printed ephemera of May 1968 in Paris, and documentary photographs. The act of presenting any Situationist material ... might be considered tantamount to incarceration, commodfying the theory (and the attendant objects) the basic underlying rhetoric of which contained the most forceful anti-commodification critique of the mid twentieth century" — Sussman, pp. 9-10.

59.
Thomas, M. J. Urban Situationism. *Planning Outlook*. (17), 1975, pp. 27-39.
An early and useful example of the typical academic reaction to the S.I., namely the summarizing of concepts and their adoption by particular professions, here urbanism and city planning. Includes a discussion of Giles Ivain Chtcheglov's 'Formula for a new city', (published in *I.S.* in 1958) and the text 'Unitary urbanism', 1961 by Vaneigem and Kotànyi.

60.

Ulmer, Gregory L. 'A night at the text': Roland Barthes's Marx Brothers. *Yale French Studies.* (73), 1987, pp. 38-57.

Includes the chapter, 'A situationist pedagogy' pp. 49-57. "Roland Barthes's approach to the gap separating the discourse of everyday life from specialized language was to enter discourse at still another level — to find a third manner of speaking capable of taking the other two into account. One of the principal tasks of my essay is to identify this alternative level, to describe the mode of entry that Barthes made posssible, and to argue that it has special value for teachers." — Ulmer, p. 38. He goes on to discuss the Situationist's attitude towards academics and proposes a psychogeography of the academy. "The formation of a new pedagogy, based on textuality and the situationist experience, will require taking seriously the program of a realized art and the practice of détournement." — Ulmer, p. 56.

61.

Walker, John A. *Glossary of art, architecture, and design since 1945.* 3rd ed. London: Library Association Publishing, 1992. [402]p., ill. ISBN 0853656398.

"A playful, volatile alliance of avant-garde artists, architects, poets, art historians and political theorists who were active in several European countries during the 1950s and '60s. In spite of their small number (70), the Situationists were to prove remarkably influential amongst Left-wing intellectuals, activists and graphic designers. ... The ideas of the Sits were drawn from surrealism, the anti-art of dada, existentialism, Marxism and anarchism. They generated countless radical pamphlets and magazines, and coined many memorable slogans. Situationist theory evolved into a kind of intellectual terrorism directed against bourgeois society and sought to overthrow by means of revolution ... Soon a conflict emerged between those members committed to art as a profession and those who sought 'the supersession of art'. The latter were convinced there could not be any such thing as 'Situationist art' because art/culture was; 'the ideal commodity, the one which helps sells all the others.'" — Walker. The glossary includes brief discussions, with short bibliographies, of the Situationists, Spur, Plagiarism, Neoism, Lettrisme, Cobra, Punk, Fluxus and Mail Art. The major reference work on Mail Art is Held Jr., John. *Mail Art: an annotated bibliography*. Metuchen: Scarecrow Press, 1991. 534 p. ISBN 0810824558.

62.
Wollen, Peter. The Situationist International. *New Left Review*. (174), March/April 1989, pp. 67-95.

Also printed in Sussman [57], pp. 20-61 "Thus the S.I. was fated to be incorporated into the legendary series of avant-garde artists and groups whose paths had intersected with popular revolutionary movements at emblematic moments. Its dissolution in 1972 brought to an end an epoch which began in Paris with the 'Futurist Manifesto of 1909 — the epoch of the historic avant-gardes with their typical apparatus of international organization and propaganda, manifestoes, congresses, quarrels, scandals, indictments, expulsions, polemics, group photographs, little magazines, mysterious episodes, provocations, utopian theories and intense desires to transform art, society, the world and the pattern of everyday life." — Wollen, p. 27 (in Sussman [57]). This is a neat summation and description of the avant-garde context from which the S.I. emerged. One of the most substantial commentaries on the movement and its heritage.

2. RELATED MOVEMENTS

2.1 LETTRISME (1946-), THE LETTRISTE INTERNATIONALE (1952-1957) AND LES LÈVRES NUES (1953-58).

63.
Foster, Stephen C. (ed.). Lettrisme: into the present. *Visible Language.* (USA) 17 (3), Summer 1983, 112 p., ill. ISSN. 00222224.

> Contents: 'Letterism: a point of views' by Stephen C. Foster, 'Chronology' by Jean-Paul Curtay, 'Letterism: a stream that runs its own course' by David W. Seaman, 'Super-writing 1983 — America 1683' by Jean-Paul Curtay, 'Approaching Letterist cinema' by Frederique Devaux, 'The limitations of Lettrisme: an interview with Henri Chopin' by Nicholas Zurbrugg, 'Selected theoretical texts from Letterists' by David W. Seaman (ed.), 'Researching Letterism and bibliography' by Pietro Ferrua, 'Exhibition checklist'. An essential introductory examination of Lettrisme. See also; Galerie Rambert (Paris, France). *Lettrisme: les debuts, 1944/1966: Isidore Isou, Gabriel Pomerand, Maurice Lemaitre, Roland Sabatier, Alain Saties: 22 Janvier/14 Fevrier 1987, Galerie Rambert, Paris.* Paris: [La Galerie], [1987]. [30]p., ill. Cover title 'Nouvel object plastique'; and Trend, David. Letters and characters — Letterism and hypergraphics: the unknown avant-garde 1945-1985. *Afterimage.* 13, Jan. 1986, pp. 6-8. Review of an exhibition at Franklin Furnace, New York.

64.
Les lèvres nues; collection complète 1954-1958. Paris: Plasma, [1978]. 600 p., ill. (Table rase).

> Facsimile edition of the 12 issues (April 1954-Sept. 1958) of this Brussels based quarterly post-surrealist journal. *Reference from Hansen [114], p. 162. Included some texts from the Lettriste Internationale members.

65.
Lettriste Internationale. *Potlatch: 1954-57.* Paris: Éditions Gérard Lebovici, 1985. 242 p. ISBN 2851841637.

> Nos. 1-29 of the Lettriste Internationale newsletter, with an introduction by Guy Debord. The journal was also reprinted in Berreby [10]. "Its

bulletin *Potlatch* (the title refers to pre-commercial societies which operate on the principle of 'the gift' rather than economic exchange) was given away. The first edition, dated 22/6/54, was produced in an edition of 50. By the end of the first series (the final issue was put out by the Situationist International rather than the LI on 5/11/57) four or five hundred copies of each issue were produced. There was only ever one issue of the second series." — Home [31], p. 20.

66.
Mariën, Marcel. *L'activité surréaliste en Belgique* (1924-1950). Bruxelles: Le Fil rouge, Editions Leber Hossmann, [1979]. 508 p., ill. (Le Fil rouge).

A large collection of facsimiles of publications resulting from surrealist activity in Belgium. It also includes a substantial bibliography covering the groups and individual bibliographies for Christian Dotremont (1922-1979), Marcel Mariën (1920-), and Paul Nougé (1895-1967).

67.
Schlatter, Christian. What is Lettrisme? *Flash Art.* (145), March/April, 1989, pp. 92-95, ill.

A flattering and concise introduction to the group. "What is Lettrisme? A historical French movement which, like the Situationists, proposed new ways of thinking, creating and inventing that rendered all preceding forms defunct." — Schlatter, p. 92. This article also includes a translation of Isidore Isou's 'Note on necrophiliac art 1962-1963.' "PAINT YOUR CADAVERS AND EXPOSE THEM. BURY YOUR PAINTINGS AND LET THEM ROT." — Isou, p. 95. Article translated by Shaun Caley.

2.2 COBRA (1948-1951).

68.
Cobra 1948-1951. Amsterdam: Van Gennep, 1980. 1 v. (various pagings), ill. (some col.).

Reprint with an introduction by Christian Dotremont of their journal: *Cobra* (1) April-June 1949 — (10) Autumn 1951, published irregularly in Amsterdam, Brussels, and Copenhagen. Text in French with some in Dutch and English. It also includes facsimiles of *Le petit Cobra* (1) 1949 — (4) Winter 1950-51.

69.
Lambert, Jean-Clarence. *Cobra*. New York: Abbeville Press, 1985.
Translated by Roberta Bailey from; *Cobra: un art libre*. Paris: Chêne/
Hachette, 1983. 262 p., ill. ISBN 2851083066. Includes a major
bibliography (pp. 249-258), a chronology, and many illustrations.
Probably the most comprehensive introductory work. Also by
Lambert see; *Cobra*. London: Sotheby Publications, 1983.

70.
Reuter, Martin. Die ästhetische und die politische Aktion: Cobra, Bauhaus
Imaginiste, Situationistische Internationale. In : *Texte zur Kunst 1957-
1982: 25 Jahre Galerie van de Loo*. München: Galerie van de Loo, 1982. 269
p., ill.
Exploration of the conflict between art and politics. This book also
includes a text by Christoph Caspari 'Liebe SPUR'. *Reference from
Bachmayer [72], p. 154.

71.
Stokvis, Willemijn. *Cobra: an international movement in art after the Second
World War*. New York: Rizzoli, 1988. 128 p., ill. ISBN 0847809250.
Translated from the Dutch by Jacob C.T. Voorthuis. General introductory
work with a select bibliography and a large illustrated section divided
nationally. Includes a translation of Constant's manifesto published in
Reflex I, Amsterdam, September — October 1948. "The dissolution of
Western classical culture is a phenomenon that can be understood only
against the background of a social evolution which can end only in the
total collapse of a principle of society thousands of years old and its
replacement by a system whose laws are based on the immediate
demands of human vitality." — Constant, p. 29. Also by Stokvis see;
Cobra prints, Cobra books. New York: Franklin Furnace, 1986.

2.3 GRUPPE SPUR (1958-1965).

72.
Bachmayer, H.M. The 'Spur' Group: on art, fun and politics. In : Schrenk,
Klaus, (ed.). *Upheavals, manifestos, manifestations: conceptions in the arts at
the beginning of the sixties: Berlin, Düsseldorf, Munich*. Köln: DuMont, 1984.
ISBN 3770116755: pp. 134-54.

A substantial essay in the catalogue of an exhibition held at the Städtische Kunsthalle Düsseldorf. Spur can be translated as either trace or trail. Their periodical *Spur* ran from 1960-1961. Bachmayer sees the group as an assimilation of the various post-war avant-gardes (from Abstract Expressionism to Cobra). He also comments on their direct connection with Kommune I in Berlin and the artist groups; Wir [We] (1959-65), Geflecht (1965-68), and Kollektiv Herzogstrasse (1975-82). On the 1962 split with the S.I. he describes how; "tension gave way to inner antagonism as again and again the divergence of art and politics brought home the prevalent incongruity of the speed of fertile imagination matched with the sluggishness of revolutionary 'Realpolitik.'" — Bachmayer, p. 141. In English and German. A facsimile edition of the collected Spur journals 1-7, (Aug. 1960 — Oct. 1961) was published as; Sturm, Helmet ... [et al.]. *Die Zeitschrift SPUR*. München: [s.n.], 1962. ca. 250 p., ill. (some col.). (Spur-Buch, Bd. 1). 270 numbered copies printed. *Reference from OCLC.

73.
Bachmayer, H.M. ... et al. *Gruppe SPUR 1958-1965, eine Dokumentation*. München: Galerie van de Loo, 1979. 210 p., ill. (some col.)
    Catalogue of an exhibition held during November 1979. Includes 'Spur-Gespräch', pp. 16-45 a conversation between Lothar Fischer, Helmut Heissenbüttel, Emil Kaufmann, Helmut Sturn, Otto van de Loo, and Hans Peter Zimmer. Includes facsimiles of all the group's manifestos. 'Spur Essay', pp. 159-173 by Emil Kaufmann. *Reference from Bachmayer [72], p. 153. The same source also refers to; Schawelka, K. Das Prinzip der Malerei und die Politik. In: *Cobra, Spur, Wir, Geflecht, Kollektiv Herzogstrasse: [Ausstellung] Galerie im Ganserhaus, Wasserburg am Inn*. München: Anderland, [1983]. [77] p., ill. Exhibition held July 31 — Sept. 15, 1983.

74.
Böckelmann, Frank and Nagel, Herbert. *Subversive Aktion, der Sinn der Organisation ist ihr Scheitern*. Frankfurt [Main]: Neue Kritik Verlag, 1976. 483 p., ill. ISBN 3801501426.
    On radicalism, intellectual life and subculture. Roberto Ohrt [45] also cites; Goeschel, Albrecht. *Richtlinien und Anschläge: Materialien zur Kritik der repressiven Gesellschaft*. [München]: C. Hanser, [1968]. 115 p. (Reihe Hanser, 9).

75.
Gruppe Spur. *Eine kultureller Putsch: Manifeste, Pamplete und Provokationen der Gruppe SPUR*. Hamburg: Nautilus, 1991. 63 p., ill. ISBN 3894011823. (Kleine Bücherei Hand und Kopf; Bd. 30).
A collection of publications by the group. For more on Gruppe Spur, Kommune I and the S.I. see; Dressen, Wolfgang, Dieter Kunzelmann and Eckhard Siepmann, (eds.). *Nilpferd des höllischen Urwalds: Spuren in eine [sic] unbekannte Stadt: Situationisten, Gruppe SPUR, Kommune I: ein Ausstellungsgeflecht des Werkbund-Archivs Berlin zwischen Kreuzberg und Scheunenviertel, November 1991*. Berlin: [Das Archiv]; Giessen: Vertrieb, Anabas Verlag, [1991]. 253 p., ill. (some col.). (Werkbund-Archiv; 24). *Reference from OCLC.

76.
Loers, Veit, (ed.). *Gruppe SPUR 1958-65: Lothar Fischer, Heimrad Prem, Helmut Sturm, H P Zimmer*. Regensberg: Städtische Galerie, 1986. 176 p., ill. ISBN 3925753036.
Catalogue of an exhibition at the Städtische Galerie Regensberg, 12 April — 25 May 1986 and the Städtische Museum Mülheim, 5 July — 24 August 1986 (also at the Museum Ulm 1987). Contents include; Spur chronologie, pp. 9-11; Künstler mit Gemüt — der Ausbruch aus der Gemütlichkeit — Veit Loers, pp. 13-28; Die Spur von der Kunst zur Situationistischen Internationale — Roberto Ohrt, pp. 33-44; and Künstlerbiographien und Bibliographien, pp. 173-176. All the text is in German. The key reference to the falling out of the Spur group and the S.I. is the following; "Prem considers that the S.I. systematically neglects its real chances in culture. It rejects favourable occasions to impose itself in existing cultural politics, whereas according to him the S.I. has no power but its power in culture — a power which could be very great and which is visibly within our reach. The S.I. majority sabotages the chances of an effective action on the terrain where it is possible. It castigates artists who would be able to succeed in doing something; it throws them out the moment they get the means to do things." — anon, at the fifth S.I. conference in Goteborg, 1961. Translated in Knabb [35], p. 89. This was originally published in *I.S.* (7) April 1962. See also; Zimmer, H.P. *H.P. Zimmer: malerier og skulpturer = Bilden und Plastiken*. Herning, Danmark: Herning Kunstmuseum, 1989. 143 p., ill. ISBN 8788367126.

77.
Roh, Juliane. The Spur Group. In: Schrenk, Klaus, (ed.). *Upheavals, manifestos, manifestations: conceptions in the arts at the beginning of the sixties: Berlin, Düsseldorf, Munich.* Köln: DuMont, 1984. ISBN 3770116755: pp. 130-133.

"In its manifestos Spur reacts absurdly and ironically to capitalistic notions of life and they propagate their own way of life which is anarchic in its rejection of bourgeois conventions. What happens in the pictures, however, is not what one would have expected from reading the manifestos. A recognizable confrontation of the informal artistic expression with the banalities of the consumer world does not occur. On the contrary, Spur is concerned with the rescue of the imagination in a world taken in by technical comfort." — Roh, p. 131. Roh also states that Prem and Uwe Lausen committed suicide, Sturm [1932-] quit painting but taught art to children; "Zimmer [1936-] risked clashes with politics on his canvas [and] only Lothar Fischer [1933-] refused to let himself be thrown of balance." — Roh, p. 133. This publication also reproduces two Spur manifestos (only the second was produced while they were members of the S.I.) with English translations. They are; *'Manifest'* [Manifesto], November 1958; and *'Avantgarde ist unerwünscht!: Flugblatt der Situationistischen Internationale'*. [The *avant-garde* is undesirable!: hand-out of the Situationist International], January 1961. Another work involving Uwe Lausen [1941-]; *Uwe Lausen, Ölbilder.* [München: Galerie Gunzenhauser, 1985]. 12 p., ill. *Reference from OCLC.

3. WORKS ON OR BY EX-SITUATIONISTS

3.1 Constant [Nieuwenhuys]. 1920-

78.
Constant. *Constant*. Hague: Gemeentemuseum, 1965. 25 p., ill.
Catalogue of an exhibition 1 October — 21 November 1965. With
texts by Constant, Jos. de Gruyter and H van Haaren. Also includes
a bibliography of publications on and by Constant and a chronology
of his exhibitions. In Dutch.

79.
Constant. *Constant, schilderijen 1969-77: Stedelijk Museum Amsterdam,
17.3-7.5.1978*. Amsterdam: Stedelijk Museum, 1978. [24] p., ill. some col.
(Cat.; nr. 636).
Parallel text in Dutch and English. Includes a conversation between
Constant and Fanny Kelk, and a text by Constant that begins 'The
dogs bark, the caravan travels on..'. "The end of art is connected with
the end of slavery. Art becomes superfluous when there is collective
creativity, as in New Babylon. But without a social revolution the
slogan 'art is dead', means no more than 'the last vestige of freedom
is dead.' So down with anti-art." — Constant, p. [12].

80.
Constant. *Constant, schilderijen 1940-1980*. ['s-Gravenhage]: Haags
Gemeentemuseum, 1980. 127 p., chiefly ill. (some col.) ISBN 9012031753.
Catalogue of an exhibition that took place during September 1980.
Includes an essay 'De schilder kunst van Constant' by J.L. Locher. In
Dutch.

81.
Constant. *Constant: werk uit de periode 1975 — 1985*. Utrecht: Central
Museum, 1985.
Exhibition catalogue. For more information on Constant see the
bibliography on him in Bandini [4], pp. 360-363. See also; Constant.
New-Babylon: imaginäre Stadtlandschaften. [S.l.: sn., 1964?].
(Unpaginated), ill. Portfolio published to accompany the exhibition
held at the Museum Hans Lange, Krefeld, 31 October — 6 December,

1964; Constant. *Opstand van de homo ludens: een bundel voordrachten en artikelen.* Bussum: Paul Brand, 1969. 148 p. (Bijivijze van eksperiment); Burkamp, Gisela, (ed.). *Constant: Arbeiten auf Papier 1948-1985: Bielefelder Kunstverein e.V., 6. Oktober — 24. November 1985.* Bielefeld: Der Kunstverein, 1985. 44 p., ill.; and Honnef, Klaus, (ed.). *Constant, 1945-1983.* Köln: Rheinland-Verlag, 1986. 98 p., ill. ISBN 3792709066. (Kunst und Altertum am Rhein; Nr. 125). Catalogue of the exhibition held January 17 — March 2, 1986, at the Rheinisches Landesmuseum Bonn. *Reference from OCLC.

82.
Constant. *New Babylon.* Den Haag: Gemeentemuseum, 1974. 120 p., ill. Exhibition at the Haags Gemeentemuseum 15 June — 1 September 1974. "Constant's major contribution to Situationist theory was within the sphere of urbanism and was most fully expressed within his 'New Babylon' project which called for a playful as opposed to a functional urbanism. This he realised through the dissolution of a structured architectural landscape in favour of something fluid and subject to change, concerns that reflect the centrality of the 'derive' and of 'psychogeographie' on Situationist thinking." — Wilson, Andrew. *Documents of the avant-garde 1945-1990: catalogue 13.* London: Sam Fogg, 1991, p. 5. See also; Banham, Reyner. *Megastructure: urban futures of the recent past.* London: Thames and Hudson, 1976. 224 p., ill. ISBN 050034684.

3.2 Guy Debord. 1931-1994

83.
Berman, Russell, Pan, David and Piccone, Paul. The Society of the Spectacle 20 years later: a discussion. *Telos.* (86), Winter 1990, pp. 81-102. This discussion of Guy Debord's *Comments on the society of the spectacle* [92] was held in the Telos offices in New York City, Feb. 7, 1990. A critical look at Debord's Spectacle theses and *Comments on the society of the spectacle.* A very good antidote to those who may wish to situate Debord in an artistic milieu. This heavy 'Critical theory' informed 'discussion' provides a detailed critique from a politico-theoretical view-point. "The *Comments* may be a kind of theoretical obituary for the various ultra-Left groups that flared up briefly and

disastrously during the 1970s, in the same way that, as has been pointed out, *The society of the spectacle* and 1968 did not prefigure a new era but, rather, concluded an old one." — Piccone, p. 102.

84.

Debord, Guy and Sanguinetti, Gianfranco. *La véritable scission dans l'Internationale*. Paris: Éditions Champ Libre, 1972. 147 p.

The first English translation was published as; *The veritable split in the international*. London: B.M. Piranha, 1974. 125 p. Described on p. 5 as "A bad translation ... virtually incomprehensible to anyone who is not an International Situationist." Second edition published March 1985 by B.M. Chronos and third edition published July 1990. "Revised and corrected throughout (by Lucy Forsyth, November 1985, and ourselves [Chronos], February 1990)." — t.p. verso. This third edition has 138 pages (ISBN 0950838020). Contents: 'Theses on the Situationist International and its time', 'Notes to serve towards the history of the S.I. from 1969-71', 'On the decomposition of our enemies', 'Report of Guy Debord to the VII Conference of the S.I. in Paris (extracts)', 'Letter of resignation of Raoul Vaneigem', 'Communiqué of the S.I. concerning Vaneigem'. "The Situationist International imposed itself in a moment of universal history as the thought of the collapse of a world; a collapse which has now begun before our eyes." — Sanguinetti and Debord, p. 11.

85.

Debord, Guy. *Oeuvres cinématographiques complètes: 1952-1978*. Paris: Éditions Champ Libre, 1978. 290 p., ill. ISBN 2851840983.

Contains the complete collection of Debord's five film scripts: *Hurlements en faveur de Sade*, 1952; *Sur le passage de quelques personnes à travers une assez courte unité de temps*, 1959; *Critique de la séparation*, 1961; *La société du spectacle*, 1973; *Réfutation de tous les jugements, tant élogieux qu'hostiles, qui ont été jusqu'ici portés sur le film 'La société du spectacle*, 1975; and *In girum imus nocte et consumimur igni*, 1978, all include visual descriptions. Translations of *On the passage of a few persons through a rather brief period of time*, 1959 and *Critique of separation*, 1961 can be found in Knabb [35], pp. 29-34. For a full translation of *In Girum...* see below [96] and the recently published *Society of the spectacle and other films* [97]. Italian translation by Paolo Salvadori as; *Opere cinematografiche complete, 1952-1978*. Rome: Arcana

Editrice, 1980. There is also a German translation of; Debord, Guy. *Contre le cinéma*. Aarhus: Scandinave de vandalisme comperé, 1964 87 p. published as; *Gegen den Film / Filmskripte*. Hamburg: Nautilus, [n.d.] *Reference from Ohrt [45], p. 335.

86.

Debord, Guy. *Préface à la quatrième édition italienne de 'la société du spectacle.'* Paris: Éditions Champ Libre, 1979. 40 p. ISBN 2851841025.

Translated by Michel Prigent and Lucy Forsyth as; *Preface to the fourth Italian edition of 'The society of the spectacle'*. London: Chronos Publications, 1979 (2nd edition 1983, 23 p. ISBN 0950838012). "This is an English edition of the preface to a translation of *La Société du spectacle* by Paola Salvadori, published by Nuova Vallecchi, Florence." t.p. verso. "I believe that there is nobody in the world capable of being interested in my book apart from those who are enemies of the existing social order and who act efficaciously starting from this position." — Debord, p. 6. "The days of this society are numbered; its reasons and its merits have been weighed in the balance and found wanting; its inhabitants are divided into two parties, one of which wants this society to disappear." — Debord, p. 23. A characteristically immodest reflection on the Situationist's 'book of theory'. Also published as an excerpt; The state of the spectacle. *Semiotext [e]*. III (3), 1988, pp. 96-98. Translated by Wendy Greenberg and John Johnston.

87.

Debord, Guy. *Textes rares: 1955-1970*. Paris: [s.n.], 1981.

Includes 'Pour le débat d'orientation du printemps 1970: note sur la première série de textes.' pp. 34-36. "Each film could give one or two Situationists working as assistants the opportunity to master their own style in this language; and the inevitable success of our works would also provide the economic base for the future production of these comrades. *The expansion of our audience is of decisive importance.*" — Debord, p. 36. *Reference from Levin [100], p. 77. See also; Brau, Éliane. *Le Situationnisme ou la nouvelle internationale*. Paris: Debresse, 1968. 198 p., ill. (Collection Révolte, no. 3). Bibliography: pp. 172-185. *Reference from OCLC.

88.

Debord, Guy. *Ordures et décombres daballes à la sortie du film "in girum imus nocte et consumimur igni"*. Paris: Éditions Champ Libre 1982.

> Reprints of 14 reviews of film, not included are; Jauffret, Regis. *Art Press*. Summer 1981, no. 50, p. 34; and Logette, Lucien, *Jeune Cinema*. Sept. — Oct. 1981, no. 137, pp. 23-25. *Reference from Levin [100], p. 125.

89.

Debord, Guy. *Considération sur l'assassinat de Gérard Lebovici*. Paris: Éditions Gérard Lebovici, 1985. [110]p., ill. ISBN 2851841564.

> Consists mainly of reprints of press coverage and comments by Debord on the assassination. "Debord's patron and friend Gérard Lebovici — a French film producer whom [Debord] met in 1971 — not only supported Debord's work by financing what was effectively a situationist press, Champ Libre, he also bought a cinema — the Studio Cujas in St. Germain — which projected Debord's cinematographic production on a continuous and exclusive basis. But only up to 1985 when suddenly, following the mysterious assassination of Lebovici in a parking lot off the Champs Elysées, Debord withdrew his films in a grand, classically situationist melodramatic gesture: outraged by the murder of his friend and by the manner in which the press reported it [in effect, blaming it on Debord as 'bad company' and spuriously linking Debord to the French terrorist group Action directe — Marcus] Debord [wrote] a book." — Tom Levin as quoted in Marcus [42], p. 452. There may also have been an English publication entitled *Apparent truth about the assassination of Gérard Lebovici*. 1984. 12 p. *Reference from Barry Pateman correspondence. The following is a short quote from an unpublished translation of the text. "I have always neglected the Press. I have never tried to exercise a right to reply, and less still have I wished to initiate a lawsuit against those who have never ceased to defame me, for as long as I can remember. But it had never been said that I had murdered, or initiated the murder of a friend."

90.

Debord, Guy and Becker-Ho, Alice. *Le 'Jeu de la guerre': relevé des positions successives de toutes les forces au cours d'une partie*. Paris: Éditions Gérard Lebovici, 1987. 160 p., ill. ISBN 2851841734.

> "We find a detailed account of a [war] game he played with Alice Becker-Ho. The game is not marked by aggression. Ponderously and

slowly the armies move their explosive mixture over the glass floor, allowing the geometric lightning of their now abstract threats of destruction to flash for only a few seconds ... To Debord's irritation the game cannot be subject to external accident. Neither wind nor weather..." — Ohrt [102], p. 17.

91.

Debord, Guy. *Society of the spectacle*. [London]: Rebel Press and Aim Publications, 1987. [unpaginated, 221 theses].

Translated from; *La société du spectacle*. Paris: Buchet-Chastel, 1967. 176 p.; and Éditions Champ Libre, 1971. 143 p. Also editions by Champ Libre published in 1983 (170 p.) and 1987 (170 p. ISBN 2851840304). Latest French edition published, somewhat ironically, by the prestigious Gallimard, 1992 (167 p. ISBN 207072803X). First English translation by Black and Red, Detroit in 1970 by Fredy Perlman, source Raspaud & Voyer [48], then revised and re-published in 1973, 1977 and 1983. There is also a translation by Donald Nicholson-Smith (1990), unpublished, which Sadie Plant [47] used for her book. The official German version was translated by Jean-Jacques Raspaud as; *Die Gesellschaft des Spektakels*. Hamburg: Nautilus, 1978. The situationist 'book of theory', "... a lapidary totalization of Situationist theory that combined the Situationist analysis of culture and society within the framework of a theoretical approach and terminology drawn from Georg Lukàc's *History and Class Consciousness* (published in France by the Arguments group...) and the political line of council communism, characteristic of Socialisme ou barbarie but distinctly recast by Debord." — Wollen, p. 26 in Sussman [57]. For a sample of S ou B see; Curtis, David Ames, (ed. & trans.). *Cornelius Castoriadis: political and social writings*. Minneapolis: University of Minneapolis, 1988. For an account of the Arguments group see; Poster, Mark. *Existential Marxism in post-war France: from Sartre to Althusser*. Princetown, N.J.: Princetown University Press, 1975.

92.

Debord, Guy. *Commentaires sur la société du spectacle*. Paris: Éditions Gérard Lebovici, 1988. 97 p. ISBN 2851842102.

Recently republished by; Paris: Gallimard, 1992. 112 p. ISBN 2070728072. Translated by Malcolm Imrie as; *Comments on the society of the spectacle*. London: Verso, 1990. 94 p. ISBN 0860913023 hbk and

0860915204 pbk. There was also a pirate edition published in Sheffield: The Pirate Press, 1991. "Since art is dead, it has evidently become extremely easy to disguise police as artists. When the latest imitations of a recuperated neo-dadaism are allowed to pontificate proudly in the media, and thus also to tinker with the decor of official palaces, like court jesters to the king, it is evident that by the same process a cultural cover is guaranteed for every agent or auxiliary of the state's networks of persuasion. Empty pseudo-museums, or pseudo-research centres on the work of nonexistent personalities, can be opened just as fast as reputations are made for journalist-cops, historian-cops, or novelist-cops." — Debord, 'Comment' XXVIII Reviewed by Paul McDonald in *Screen*. 32(4), Winter 1991, pp. 491-494.

93.
Debord, Guy. Raport sur la construction des situations et sur les conditions de l'organisation et de l'action de la tendance situationniste internationale. In: Musée national d'art moderne, Galeries contemporaires. *Sur le passage de quelques personnes à travers une assez courte unité de temps: à propos de l'Internationale situationniste, 1957 — 1972*. Paris: Centre Georges Pompidou, 1989. [5], 20, [6] p. ISBN 2858505217.

Mirror-finish cover. Also exhibition catalogue for the exhibition at the Musée national d'art moderne, Centre Georges Pompidou, Paris, France, February 21, 1989 — April 9, 1989. Text first published in 1957.

94.
Debord, Guy. The Situationists and the new forms of action in politics or art. In: Sussman, Elisabeth, (ed). *On the passage of a few people through a rather brief moment in time: the Situationist International 1957-1972*. Boston, Mass.: M.I.T. Press; Institute of Contemporary Art, Boston, 1989, pp. 148-153.

Translated by Thomas Y. Levin and first published in; *Destruktion af RSG-6: En kollektiv manifestation af Situationistisk International*. Odense, Denmark: Galerie EXI, 1963, pp. 15-18. Also reprinted in Debord. *Textes rares: 1957-1970*. Paris: [s.n.], 1981, pp. 18-22. 'RSG' refers to 'Regional Seat of Government' and derives from a publication by the English 'Spies for Peace' called *Danger: official secret-RSG 6*. Also translated in Sussman [57] is 'Two accounts of the dérive', pp. 135-139, first published as 'Deux comptes rendus de dérive'. *Les lèvres nues*. (9) November 1956, pp. 10-13.

95.

Debord, Guy. *Panegyric: volume 1.* London: Verso, 1991. 79 p. ISBN 086091559X pbk.

Translation by James Brook of *Panégyrique I.* Paris: Éditions Gérard Lebovici, 1989. ISBN 2851842242. A short piece of autobiographical prose with little informational value but much musing on, amongst other things, drinking and war. "Before the age of twenty, I saw the peaceful part of my youth come to an end; and I now had nothing left except the obligation to pursue all my tastes without restraint, though in difficult conditions. I headed first towards that very attractive milieu where an extreme nihilism no longer wanted to know about nor, above all, continue what had previously been considered the use of life or the arts" — Debord, p. 15.

96.

Debord, Guy. *In girum imus nocte et consumimur igni.* London: Pelagian Press, 1992. 84 p., ill. ISBN 0948688068.

This was also published in France under the same title (but in French) by; Éditions Gérard Lebovici, 1990. 74 p. ISBN 2851842226. The English edition has a preface and translation by Lucy Forsyth. This is a complete translation of the original 1978 edition, including camera directions, 24 film stills and footnotes added by Debord in 1991. "In this sense I have loved my epoch, which will have seen existing security vanish, and everything which was socially ordained melt away." — Debord. The text is interesting because it highlights, in distinction to Debord's more revolutionary and avant-garde texts, a melancholic nostalgia for 'a lost Paris'. Partial translation also appeared in *Block.* (14), Autumn 1988, pp. 30-37, ill. Incomplete German translation as; *Wir irren des Nachts im Kreis uber und werden vom Feuer verzebrt.* Berlin: Edition Tiamat, 1985. The palindrome translates as; "We go round and round in the night and are consumed by fire."

97.

Debord, Guy. *Society of the spectacle and other films.* London: Rebel Press, 1992. 136 p., ill. ISBN 0946061068.

Collected English translations of the first five films by Guy Debord. Includes a short introduction by Richard Parry mostly concerned with the reasons behind Debord's current refusal to show any of his films. This book along with *In Girum...* [96] means that all the films in *Qeuvres cinématographiques complètes* [85] have now been translated.

98.
Forsyth, Lucy. In girum imus nocte et consumimur igni. *Block*. (14), Autumn, 1988, pp. 27-37, ill.

Subtitled "Introduction: the post-war cultural avant-garde in Europe." General discussion of Situationist concepts and explanation about the context of the film and its translation. *In girum imus nocte consumimur igni* was Debord's last film made by Simar Films in 1978 and was shown in France up to 1984 where it was withdrawn upon the murder of Gérard Lebovici. The full text of the film was going to be published by Chronos Publications in 1989, but has since been published by Pelagian Press, 1992.

99.
Jenny, Laurent. The unrepresentable enemy. *Art & Text*. (Australia), (35), Summer 1990, pp. 108-12, ill.

A wide-ranging and confusing review of Debord's *Commentaires sur la société du spectacle* [92]. "The effects of exile are felt in the very style of the watchman: obsessed with perhaps insignificant details, he has acquired a classical coldness and haughty aloofness, but this is also because he has been driven to reserve and ruse by the omnipresence of spies. For him, writing is but another way of surveying a desolate shore while taking shots at the unrepresentable enemy with the last cartridges of metaphysics." — Jenny, p. 112.

100.
Levin, Thomas Y. Dismantling the spectacle: the cinema of Guy Debord. In : Sussman, Elisabeth, (ed). *On the passage of a few people through a rather brief moment in time: the Situationist International 1957-1972*. Boston, Mass.: M.I.T. Press; Institute of Contemporary Art, Boston, 1989, pp. 72-123, ill.

An exhaustive account of the relationship between Debord and the cinema. Includes an extract from a letter from Debord to Levin (dated 24 April 1989): "It seems to me that my work [in the cinema], very succinct but extended over a period of twenty-six years, did indeed correspond to the principal criteria of modern art: (1) a very marked originality from the start and the firm decision never to do 'the same thing' two times in a row, while still maintaining a personal style and a set of thematic concerns that are always easily recognizable; (2) an understanding of contemporary society, *id est* explaining it by criticizing it, since ours is a time which is distinctly lacking less in apologetics than in criticism; (3) finally, to have been revolutionary *in form as well as in content*, something which always struck me as following the direction of all the 'unitary' aspirations of modern art, toward the point where that art attempted to go beyond art." — Debord, p. 109. Levin also reproduces a publicity leaflet produced by Simar films to publicise La société du spectacle, 1973. For an account of French experimental cinema and Debord's place within it see; Noguez, Dominique. *Éloge du cinéma expérimental: définitions, jalons, perspectives.* Paris: Musée nationale d'art moderne, Centre Georges Pompidou, 1979. 189 p., ill. ISBN 2858500835.

101.
Marcus, Greil. Guy Debord's Mémoires: a Situationist primer. In : Sussman, Elisabeth, (ed). *On the passage of a few people through a rather brief moment in time: the Situationist International 1957-1972.* Boston, Mass.: M.I.T. Press; Institute of Contemporary Art, Boston, 1989, pp. 124-131, ill.
An essay on the book *Mémoires*. "*Mémoires* is all fragments: hundreds of snippets of text from travel literature, poems, histories, novels, tracts on political economy, film scripts, newspapers, magazines, sociological treatises, plus whole or partial photographs, cartoons, comic strips, maps, building plans, advertisements, old etchings and woodcuts, all overlaid by colored lines, patterns, and splotches painted by Asger Jorn. Refusing the valorization of original speech, the book nevertheless seems to speak with a unique and unknown tongue... In the combinations of its found, scavenged, or stolen materials, *Mémoires* affirms that everything needed to say whatever one might want to say is already present, accessible to anyone; the book defines a project, and tells a story."—Marcus, p. 126. An unauthorised edition of *Mémoires* is said to have been published by; Milan: Multhipa Edizioni, 1975. 60 p. (Multhipa Reprint). *Reference from Hansen [114], p. 156.

102.
Ohrt, Roberto. *If I wasn't Alexander I would like to be Diogenes.* [Hamburg?]: [s.n.], 1987. 17 p.
First published in *Durch.* (Austria), (3-4), Nov. 1987, pp. 27-48. Translated by Ian Brunskill in the same issue and subsequently

published as a pamphlet. It follows the career of Debord from the time of his life in Paris at the age of 20 till his publication with Alice Becker-Ho of *Le 'Jeu de la Guerre'* [90]. Concentrates chiefly on Debord's uneasy relationship with art and artists.

103.
Peters, Mike. The secret articles of Guy Debord. *Here and Now*. (7/8), 1989, pp. 32-33.

A short review of Debord's *Commentaries sur la société du spectacle*. [92] "... Situationism has been indexed, filed, stored, and hedged around with superstitious gossip, so that it is impossible for Debord to escape the aura of his name in what passes as the 'history' of these times ... it would be impossible to expect from Debord's latest text anything approaching an explanation of these developments." — Peters, p. 32.

104.
Richards, Thomas. *The commodity culture of Victorian England: advertising and spectacle 1851 — 1914*. Stanford: Stanford University Press, 1990. xiv, 306 p., ill. ISBN 0804716528.

Published in Britain by Verso in 1991. "This book is intended to take up the analysis where Debord leaves it off [in *The society of the spectacle*], for at the time Debord saw it at work in France, the commodity spectacle was already one hundred years old. The spectacle and the style of mass advertising that it engendered were products of Victorian commodity culture, and they must be seen, to use Debord's words, as 'both the result and the project of the existing mode of production.'" — Thomas, p. 14. Includes critical application of Debord related concepts.

3.3 Asger Jorn. 1914-1973.

105.
Andersen, Troels. Asger Jorn and the Situationist International. In: Sussman, Elisabeth, (ed). *On the passage of a few people through a rather brief moment in time: the Situationist International 1957-1972.* Boston, Mass.: M.I.T. Press; Institute of Contemporary Art, Boston, 1989, pp. 62-66, ill.

Brief run through of Jorn's connections with various post-war avant-garde groups and in particular mentions the formative influence of the Danish anarco-syndicalist leader, Christian Christensen. Andersen corroborates the fact that Jorn financed the S.I. journal from 1958 to mid 1961 when he was, as he put it 'demissioned'. However, Andersen states that he "continue[d] to financially support the magazine for some time to come." — p. 64. Andersen also recounts that; "Debord received a fine sample of these ironic and sharp paintings [from the exhibition 'Modifications' (1959) and 'Nouvelles défigurations' (1962)] as a gift from Jorn." — p. 66. See also; Andersen, Troels. *Asger Jorn, 1914-1973: katalog over arbejder tilhørende Silkeborg Kunstmuseum.* Silkeborg: Silkeborg Kunstmuseum, 1974. ca. 150 p., ill. In Danish and English.

106.
Atkins, Guy, (with the help of Troels Andersen). *Jorn in Scandinavia, 1930-1953.* London: Lund Humphries, 1968. 418 p., ill. (some col.).

"A study of Asger Jorn's artistic development from 1930 to 1953 and a catalogue of his oil paintings from that period." — t.p. First volume of Jorn's catalogue raisonné.

107.
Atkins, Guy, (with the help of Troels Andersen). *Asger Jorn: the crucial years, 1954-1964.* London: Lund Humphries, 1977. 369 p., ill. (some col.). ISBN 853313989.

"A study of Asger Jorn's artistic development from 1954 to 1964 and a catalogue of his oil paintings from that period." — t.p. Of particular interest to our subject are the chapters 'Situationists (1957-61)', pp. 51-63 and 'Modifications and disfigurations (1959-62)', pp. 65-70. The former states the influence of Jorn on the recruitment of members and interprets his resignation as signalling the fragmentation of the movement. Includes reproductions, some in colour, of all the modifications series known at that time.

108.
Atkins, Guy, (with the help of Troels Andersen). *Asger Jorn: the final years, 1965-1973.* London: Lund Humphries, 1980. 241 p., ill. (some col.). ISBN 853314381.

"A study of Asger Jorn's artistic development from 1965 to 1973 and a catalogue of his oil paintings from that period." — t.p. Includes a chapter by Frank Whitford 'Collages and décollages' which briefly discusses the Jorn/Debord collaborations. "The most striking images in both books are those derived from advertisements and comic strips, mined from the rich seam of popular culture and mass consumerism." — Whitford, p. 67. It should also be noted that all the books in this series were designed by Herbert Spenser and the colour plates printed by Jorn's favourite printers Permild & Rosengreen of Copenhagen.

109.
Atkins, Guy, (with the help of Troels Andersen). *Asger Jorn: supplement to the oeuvre catalogue of his paintings from 1930 to 1973.* London: The Asger Jorn Trust in association with Lund Humphries, 1986. 70 p., ill. ISBN 853314977.

Contains new descriptions of 100 paintings that had come to light since the last publication in the series of 1980. Reproductions include a collaboration with Yves Klein, Ralph Rumney and Walasse Ting (1956), a collaboration with Pinot-Gallizio (1957), five unfinished modifications (c.1962) and one unfinished modification (1964).

110.
Birtwistle, Graham. *Living art: Asger Jorn's comprehensive theory of art between Helhesten and Cobra (1946-1949).* Utrecht: Reflex, 1986. viii, 285 p., ill. ISBN 9063221274.

"This extremely important book gives a comprehensive account of Jorn's thought and writings during the formative pre-Cobra years and offers a number of insights on how these developed later. It draws extensively on both published and unpublished manuscripts." — Wollen, p. 60 in Sussman [57].

111.
Diederichsen, Diedrich. Asger Jorn. *Artscribe.* (66), Nov./Dec. 1987, pp. 55-58, ill.

An overview of the art and life of Asger Jorn, a man who; "seems compelled to found movement after movement ... Jorn's collages, his experiments with torn posters, with over-painting and spray painting, all date from this phase of his activity with the Situationist International, where painting was obviously called into question." — Diederichsen, p. 56. Diedrich Diederichsen is the editor of *Spex Magazine* based in Cologne.

112.
Fuchs, Anneli Nordbrandt. Asger Jorn's 'modifikationer': til belysning af situationismens aestetik. *Kunst og Kultur.* (Norway), 65 (2), 1982, pp. 86-93, ill.
An extensive article concerning Jorn's détournement of 'flea market' paintings. Includes reproductions of the paintings 'Le lac des canards', 1959 and 'Détournement de paysage', 1959. In Norwegian.

113.
Gombin, Richard. The critique of Marxist reification. In: *The radical tradition: a study in modern revolutionary thought.* London : Methuen, 1978. ISBN 0416661505: pp. 119-125.
"[Jorn] foresees the replacement of authoritarian socialism by its contrary: a value liberating society. According to this dialectic, a world of creation will follow upon the world of economy. In this new world, Jorn concludes, the changing of the conditions of existence will be the works of the producers themselves, become creators." —Gombin, pp. 124-125.

114.
Hansen, Per Hofmann. *A bibliography of Asger Jorn's writings.* Silkeborg: Silkeborg Kunstmuseum and the Asger Jorn Foundation, 1988. 189 p., ill. ISBN 8787932202.
A superb piece of research into the publications of Asger Jorn. With over 739 entries and essays by Per Hofman Hansen and Peter Shield ('On reading Asger Jorn', pp. 35-38), this is a vital reference tool not only for research into Jorn but also for the many groups he was associated with, such as Cobra and the S.I. The bibliography covers the period 1932-1985 and is divided into three sections 'Jorn's books: a chronological survey', 'Jorn's collected printed output', and 'A concordance'. Needless to say this book contains many references not included in this bibliography. Parallel text in Danish and English. Translated by Peter Shield.

115.
Jorn, [Asger]. *Le jardin d'Albisola.* Torino: Edizioni d'arte Fratelli Pozzo, 1974. [48] p., chiefly ill.
Preface by Ezio Gribaudo. Text also by Alberico Salla. Contains essay 'De l'architecture sauvage' by Guy Debord which has also been translated as 'On wild architecture' by Thomas Y. Levin for Sussman [57], on pp. 174-175. The book is a chiefly photographic guide to Jorn's garden sculpture and decoration at Albisola. Text in Italian.

116.
Jorn, Asger and Debord, Guy. *Fin de Copenhague*. Paris: Éditions Allia, 1985. [45] p., chiefly ill. ISBN 2904235068.

Originally published in an edition of 200 by the Bauhaus Imaginiste (Copenhagen: Permild & Rosengreen, 1957). It is also included in facsimile in Berreby [10], pp. 553-92. "Overpainted collage satire of advertising, mass media, and city planning, purportedly assembled and printed in forty-eight hours on the basis of a single visit to a single newsstand; rough sketch for Debord's *Mémoires*." —Marcus [42], p. 455.

117.
Jorn, Asger. Detourned Painting. In: Sussman, Elisabeth, (ed). *On the passage of a few people through a rather brief moment in time: the Situationist International 1957-1972*. Boston, Mass.: M.I.T. Press; Institute of Contemporary Art, Boston, 1989, pp. 140-142, ill.

Short text translated by Thomas Y. Levin first published as 'Peinture détourné' in *Vingt peintures modifées par Asger Jorn*. Paris: Galerie Rive Gauche, 1959. "Intended for the general public. Reads effortlessly: Be modern, collectors, museums. If you have old paintings, do not despair. Retain your memories but detourn them so that they correspond with your era. Why reject the old if one can modernize it with a few strokes of the brush? This casts a bit of contemporaneity on your old culture. Be up to date, and distinguished at the same time. Painting is over. You might as well finish it off. Detourn. Long live painting." — Jorn. For more discussion of these works see; Zweite, Armin, (ed.). *Asger Jorn 1914-1973*. München: Städtische Galerie im Lenbachaus, 1987. 285 p., ill. (some col.). ISBN 3886450732. Catalogue of an exhibition 21 January — 29 March 1987. See especially Zweite's 'Modifikationen und Defigurationen', pp. 67 — 73. Text in German.

3.4 Jørgen Nash.

118.
Magnus, Carl [1943-], Jørgen Nash, Heimrad Prem [1934-78], Hardy Strid [1921-], and Jens Jørgen Thorsen [1932-]. *Situationister i konsten*. [Örkelljunga: Bauhaus situationiste, 1966]. [ca.100] p., ill.

An excellent introduction to the history of the Second Situationist International. Chiefly in Swedish, Danish and German but includes an English introduction by Patric O'Brian [Asger Jorn]. "The anti-art of the late 1950s and early sixties stated that visual art was a useless medium for creativity and thinking. It was the radiation of art into pure existence, into social life, into urbanism, into action and into thinking which was regarded as the important thing. The start of situationism, the foundation of the first *internationale situationniste* in 1957, was a reflection of this thinking. The motto 'Réaliser la Philosophie' [sic] was a starting point for situationist anti-art. But it caused also violent discussions in the first situationist international. Opposing this point of view, Strid, Nash and Thorsen among others in 1962 founded the Second Internationale situationniste. These five situationists, Strid, Prem, Thorsen, Magnus, Nash, are all aiming to place art in new social connections. They are fully aware of the possibilities of artistic radiation. Far from creating any feeling of anti-art in their minds, this point of view gives visual arts a far more central position in their experiments." — Jorn, p. 1. Each artist is given a section of the book. Here they provide biographical details, examples of their work and some commentary. Thorsen has this to say about Debord; "The Gup [sic] Debord theory stated that by passing rapidly through completely unknown surroundings of labyrintic caracter [sic], people should be forced into a 'verfremdungs' —situation wanting to express new whishes [sic] for a new urbanism. Labyrinths of this sort were named Derive-Labyrinths. To me this theory always seemed nonsense." — Thorsen, in the text 'The communication state in art'. Also included is the 'Co-Ritus-Manifest' 1961 signed by Thorsen, Nash, Strid, and Ambrosius Fjord. Thorsen along with Nash edited a book; *Situationister 1957-70.* Vanlöse, Eksp.: Concord, Jyllingevej 2, 1970. [180] p., ill. "Redaktion: Ambrosius Fjord, Patric O'Brien." — title page. *Reference from OCLC. Thorsen has also had a collection of essays published as; *Friheden er ikke til salg: synspunkter og essays samlet under et berufsverbot.* [Köbenhavn]: Bogan, 1980. 192 p., ill. ISBN 8787533545. For a biography of Hardy Strid and a portrait of the Swedish milieu see; Sellem, Jean. *Hardy Strid's work and Swedish modernism in art from 1935 to 1980.* Munich: Omnibus Press, 1981. 224p., ill. ISBN 3923091001.

119.

Morell, Lars. *Poesien breder sig: Jørgen Nash, Drakabygget & Situationisterne.* Köbenhavn: Det kongelige Bibliotek, 1981. 128p., ill. ISBN 8770233675. A substantial monograph on the career of Jørgen Nash containing many black and white photographs previously un-published. Text in Danish. *Drakabygget* [Dragon's lair] was the name of Nash's farm and the title of a periodical he edited, along with Katarina Lindell, between 1962-4 ("for five or six issues" — Atkins [107], p. 60). For a book by another leading figure of the Second Situationist International see; Thorsen, Jens Jørgen. *Modernisme i dansk kunst: specielt efter 1940.* [Copenhagen]: Thaning & Appel, 1965. 182 p., ill. ; and Thorsen, Jens Jørgen. *Modernisme i dansk malerkunst.* [Copenhagen]: P. Fogtdal, 1987. 351 p., ill. ISBN 8772480238. Also associated with the second international was Jacqueline de Jong who edited the journal *Situationist Times.* (1-6) 1962 — 1967. "The *Situationist Times* was originally intended as an orthodox Situationist periodical to run alongside IS, but at Gothenburg it was decided that a second paper would be too expensive, besides presenting the problem of translation into English. Jacqueline de Jong, after her expulsion, launched and edited the magazine single handed, though many of the photographs and ideas were supplied by Jorn. Two heavily illustrated issues of *The Situationist Times* (on knots and labyrinths) attained a respectable size of around 200 pages and a print run of 1,600 copies." — Atkins [107], p. 62. The journal was edited by de Jong from her retreat in Hengelo. No. 4 (1963) was a special issue on spirals and labyrinths, with texts by Gaston Bachelard and Gordon Fazakerley (who had also collaborated with Nash on; Fazakerley, Gordon. *Drawings, poems.* Drakabygget: Bauhaus Situationniste, 1962. 36 p., ill.). No. 5 (1964) concentrated on rings and chains and no. 6 (1967) was a collection of lithographs by artists including Alechinsky and Jorn. Also by de Jong; *Jacqueline de Jong: nieuw werk.* Amsterdam: Éditions Vincent Steinmetz, 1987. *Reference from Ohrt [45], p. 320. A recent publication, with masses of information on the lesser known Situationists is: Bauhaus Situationist. *Lund Art Press.* 2 (3), 1992, 244 p., ill. ISSN 11015462.

120.
Nash, Jørgen and Jorn, Asger. Stavrim, sonetter. In: Nash, Jørgen. *Her er jeg: samlede digte 1942-75.* Köbenhavn: Hernov, 1975. ISBN 8772157968: pp. 165-210.

A version of a collaborative work produced when both artists were members of the S.I. First edition; Köbenhavn: Permild & Rosengreen, 1960, [59] p., ill.; second edition, abridged and re-edited; Köbenhavn: Gyldendal, 1966. [46] p., ill. Other works by Nash include; *Græsrodens sange: pluk fra poesialbum 1942-90.* [Copenhagen]: Tilderneskifter, 1990. 183 p., ill. ISBN 8774454129. Illustrated by Asger Jorn; and *Springkniven: tekster fra kulturrevolutionen.* Köbenhavn: Hernov, 1976. 221 p., ill. ISBN 8772158263.

3.5 Pinot-Gallizio, Giuseppe. 1902-1964.

121.
Bandini, Mirella, and Passoni, Aldo, (eds.). *Pinot-Gallizio e il Laboratorio sperimentale d'Alba del Movimento internazionale per una Bauhaus immaginista (1955-57) e dell'internazionale situazionista (1957-60).* Torino: Galleria civica d'arte moderna, 1974. [180] p., ill.

Catalogue of an exhibition at Turin 28 May — 15 July 1974 and at the Palazzo della Maddalena di Alba. Includes many reprints of texts by Asger Jorn. Bandini includes a 'bio-bibliography' of Pinot-Gallizio in his *L'estetico il politico...* [4], pp. 367-370. There was also a publication; *Archivo Pinot-Gallizio: Acquisizioni 1971-78, Nr. 97-99.* Turin: Galleria Civica d'Arte Moderna, May 1974. *Reference from Ohrt [45], p. 313.

122.
Bandini, Mirella. Pinot-Gallizio: il 'Primo Laboratorio di Esperienze Immaginiste del Movimento per una Bauhaus Immaginist' (Alba 1955-57) e il 'Laboratorio Sperimentale d'Alba dell'Internazionale Situazionista' (1957-60). *Data* (Italy). 3 (9), Autumn 1973, pp. 16-29, 82-85, 94-95, ill.

The article also includes a facsimile of Pinot-Gallizio's *Manifesto della pittura industriale: per un'arte unitaria applicabile.* Dal Laboratorio Situazionista di Alba Agosto, 1959. This was first published in the bulletin of the Notizie Gallery in Turin (directed by Elio Benoldi, Enrico Crispolti and Luciano Pistoi) no. 9, October 1959 and in *Internationale situationniste* (3) December 1959. Also reproduced is Asger Jorn's *La fine dell'economia e la realizzazione dell'arte*, 1960, [pp. 26-29]; both of these are in Italian. Pages 82-85 are an English translation of Bandini's text while pages 94-95 are a French translation. The article documents Pinot-Gallizio's involvement with the rise and fall of the Bauhaus Imaginiste, the formation of the Situationist International (1957), his becoming (with his son, Giors Melanotte) one of the few Italian members, and his eventual expulsion in 1960. It also chronicles the showing of the artist's 'industrial paintings' and 'the cavern of anti-material'. Bandini argues forcefully for the recognition that Pinot-Gallizio was an influential member of the post-war European avant-garde.

123.
Bandini, Mirella. An enormous and unknown chemical reaction: the experimental laboratory in Alba. In : Sussman, Elisabeth, (ed). *On the passage of a few people through a rather brief moment in time: the Situationist International 1957-1972*. Boston, Mass.: M.I.T. Press; Institute of Contemporary Art, Boston, 1989, pp. 67-71.

Short text recounting much of the same material that had gone into the *Data* [122] text above. The phrase "an enormous and unknown chemical reaction" was the prophetic notes made by Pinot-Gallizio in his diary after the First World Conference of Free Artists in 1956.

124.
Gallizio, Pinot. *Pinot-Gallizio: le situationnisme et la peinture: du 13 février au 4 mars 1989, Galerie 1900-2000*. Paris: M. Fleiss, 1989. 40 p., ill. (12 col.)

Exhibition catalogue. Galerie 1900-2000, Marcel Fleiss, 8, Rue Bonaparte 75006 Paris. Includes extracts from text by Renato Barilli, Michèle Bernstein, Giuseppe Bonini, Maurizio Calvesi, Luigi Carluccio, Renato Gallizio, Renzo Guasco, Asger Jorn and Carlo Lonzi. As well as reproductions of Gallizio's paintings the catalogue contains documentary photographs and stills from a film by Gil and Charlotte Wolman.

3.6 Ralph Rumney. 1934-

125.
Garlake, Margaret. Ralph Rumney. *Art Monthly*. (125), April, 1989, p. 17.

Review of the exhibition at England & Co, London, March 9 — 25, 1989. "The title [The map is not the territory (1985)] can stand as a metaphor for Rumney's relationship with a certain territory in 20th-century art. His relationship with the avant-garde has been, while continuous, a constant questioning of its intentions. His concern has been with ideas, with the purposes that can be served by art, rather than with artefacts, a situation in which innovation is not the prime objective of the work." — Garlake, p. 17.

126.
Rumney, Ralph. Review of Asger Jorn: the crucial years 1954-1964. *Art Monthly.* (9), Jul-Aug. 1977, pp. 18-19.

A positive and brief review of both the book [107] and Jorn's life. "Despite his many other activities, including his onerous involvement with the Situationist International of which he was one of the founders, the fact that apart from prints and tapestries and what is probably the largest ceramic mural of its kind in the world, he also managed in this ten year period to produce a respectable body of writing even for a professional author, and at least 751 paintings gives some idea of this protean energy." — Rumney, p. 19.

127.
Rumney, Ralph. *The Map is not the territory.* Glasgow: Transmission Gallery, 1985.

Fold out A3 sheet, printed both sides, ill. Catalogue of an exhibition held at the Transmission gallery in 1985. Contains 'A biographical sketch' by Guy Atkins, 'April 1985 — Ralph Rumney' by Felix Guettary [sic?], ' [untitled]' by Jean Pierre Le Dantrec, 'Victory in Venice' by David Dunbar, and 'The image is not the reality' by Malcolm Dickson.

128.
Rumney, Ralph. [Interviewed by Stewart Home.] The Situationist International and its historification. *Art Monthly.* (127), June, 1989, pp. 3-4.

Conversation between Ralph Rumney and Stewart Home concerning the exhibition at the ICA and the rationale behind it. "What's happened now is that our work has entered the public domain and so we can't really stop museums taking an interest in it. It's there, it's history, it's recuperation, it's whatever you like." — Rumney, p. 3. This was reprinted in *Smile* (11), 1989, p. 3, minus the introduction and the footnotes.

129.
Rumney, Ralph. *Ralph Rumney: Constats 1950-1988*. London: England and Co., 1989. 12 p., ill.

> Catalogue of an exhibition held between 9 March — 25 March 1989. With text by Tony Del Renzio 'Some observations instead of a forward', pp. 6-9 and a 'Selected Chronology 1934-1989.' " [1961] ... Rumney like many of his contemporaries, was becoming disillusioned with the art market which seemed increasingly geared to repetitive painting and punishing artists for innovation or curiosity." — p. 12.

130.
Rumney, Ralph. Ralph Rumney: the *Vague* interview: 4/5/89. *Vague*. (22), 1989, pp. 27-41, ill.

> "Rather than adding to [the art historians] by covering the ICA exhibition and related books and media events, I'm just running the following interview with Ralph. It covers all that anyway." — *Vague*, p. 27. In-depth anecdotal account of Rumney's career and his involvement with the Situationists and related individuals and events. Also discusses the on going historification of the S.I.

3.7 Gianfranco Sanguinetti.

131.
Censor [Gianfranco Sanguinetti]. *Rapporto veridico sulle ultime possibilità di salvare il capitalismo in Italia*. Milan: Ugo Mursia, 1975. 139 p.

> Translates as 'True report on the last chance to save capitalism in Italy'. Translated by Debord as; *Véridique rapport sur les dernières chances de sauver le capitalisme en Italie*. Paris: Éditions Champ Libre, 1976. 185 p. Partially translated by Richard Gardner as; What the communists really are. *Semiotext[e]*. III (3), 1980, pp. 92-95. Cited in Bandini [4], p. 382 is another work by Sanguinetti; *Prove dell'inesistenza di Censor: enunciate dal suo autore*. Milan: [s.n.], 1976. 24 p.

132.
Sanguinetti, Gianfranco. *Del terrorismo e dello stato: la teoria e la practica del terrorismo per la prima volta divulgata*. Milan: [s.n.], 1979.

> Translated by Lucy Forsyth and Michel Prigent, from the French translation by Jean-François Martos (Grenoble: [s.n.], 1980. 81 p.), as;

On terrorism and the state: the theory and practice of terrorism divulged for the first time. London: B.M. Chronos, 1982. 101 p. ISBN 0950838004. This edition has an interesting foreword by Lucy Forsyth detailing some of the background to the publication and also the 1980 preface to the French Edition by Sanguinetti. Described by Bob Black; "This vigourous if not fully substantiated argument by an important situationist that Red Brigades Terrorism was orchestrated by the Italian intelligence services got the author prosecuted in his native Italy. Especially interesting in its dissection of the conservatism of the Italian Communist Party." — Black [173], reading list.

3.8 Alexander Trocchi. 1925-1984.

133.
Calder, John. Alexander Trocchi. *Edinburgh Review*. (70), 1985, pp. 32-35. Brief review of Trocchi's literary life notable for Calder's criticism of Trocchi's drug dependency. Describes Sigma as; "an excuse to avoid getting on with a sequel to *Cain's Book* ... It is not as a cosmonaut of inner space that Trocchi has a chance of being remembered, but as a descriptive writer able to create an ambience, possessing a rare sense of style." — pp. 34-35. Calder & Boyars published Trocchi's first serious novel *Cain's Book*, in 1963 and defended it against charges of obscenity in 1964. This issue of the *Edinburgh Review* also included; Logue, Christopher. Alexander Trocchi and the beginning of Merlin. *Edinburgh Review*. (70), 1985, pp. 59-65.

134.
McGrath, Tom. Remembering Alex Trocchi. *Edinburgh Review*. (70), 1985, pp. 36-47.
An anecdotal account of McGrath's relationship with Trocchi with particular reference to their use of drugs. McGrath was features editor of *Peace News* and later edited *International Times*.

135.
Morgan, Edwin. Alexander Trocchi: a survey. *Edinburgh Review*. (70), 1985, pp. 48-58.
A critical survey of Trocchi's literary output including his work as a translator and his poetry. Highlights recurring themes in Trocchi's

work such as writing in the first person and the repeated use of the imagery of hanging.

136.
Scott, Andrew Murray, (ed.). *Invisible insurrection of a million minds: a Trocchi reader*. Edinburgh: Polygon, 1991. xi, 228 p. ISBN 0748661085.
Of particular interest to our subject in this compilation of 27 short texts of fiction and non-fiction is; 'The invisible insurrection of a million minds', and 'Sigma : a tactical blueprint.' "Certainly the most uncompromising attack on conventional culture was launched by Dada at the end of the First World War. But the usual defence mechanisms were soon operating: the turds of 'anti-art' were solemnly framed and hung alongside 'the School of Athens' ; Dada thereby underwent the castration by card-index and was soon safely entombed in the histories as just another school of art." — Trocchi, p. 183. There are two large collections of Trocchi's papers, one is the 'Trocchi Collection' (22 boxes) held in the archive of the Olin Library at Washington University, St Louis, Missouri. The other collection is, at present, held by the Alexander Trocchi Estate [Alexander Trocchi Archive]. This second collection holds many papers of interest concerning the links between Trocchi, the Lettriste Internationale, the Situationist International and includes letters from Guy Debord, Greil Marcus, and Christopher Gray.

137.
Scott, Andrew Murray. *Alexander Trocchi: the making of the monster*. Edinburgh: Polygon, 1991, 182 p., ill. ISBN 0748661069.
This is the first biography of Trocchi and hopefully it will not be the last. The text is ridden with inaccuracies and concentrates more on the idea of Trocchi as a writer than as a major 'all-round' influence on the fifties and Sixties underground. Scott only briefly mentions Trocchi's associations with the Situationists ("the heart of existentialism" — p. 64) and the "Lettrisme [sic] International" (p. 64). According to Murray, Trocchi wrote the following on his ex-communication from the S.I. "And exclusions were total. It meant ostracism, cutting people. Ultimately, it leads to shooting people — that's where it would have led, if Guy had ever taken over. And I couldn't shoot anyone." — p. 125.

138.

Slater, Howard. Alexander Trocchi and Project Sigma. *Variant*. (7), 1989, pp. 30-37.

Excellent introduction to Trocchi's underrated Project Sigma and the *Sigma Portfolio*. One of Trocchi's contributions was a re-writing of 'Manifesto Situationiste' for *Sigma Portfolio*. (18), 1964. "In Trocchi's Manifesto Situationisme he recognises the need for a revolutionary solution to our 'infinitely complex age of crises', taking up the 'avant-garde's' citing of the need for a collective concrete creativity involving the realization of poetry in a poetry of acts." —Slater, pp. 34. This text was also published in an unauthorised and edited version in; *Smile*. (11), 1989. There is much Sigma Portfolio and Project Sigma documentation in 'The Alexander Trocchi Archive.'

139.

Trocchi, Alexander. *Man at leisure*. London: Calder and Boyars, 1972. 90 p. ISBN 0714503576 hbk and 0714503584 pbk. (Signature series no. 15.) "Me work? Go furk!" — p.78. Contains a short introduction by William Burroughs. This was Trocchi's only collection of poems to be published. "The poems span a long period of time, and range from the lyricism of some of his early love poems, reflections on his involvement in the drug culture, to the penetrating and very pithy comment on contemporary figures and events contained in his later work." — back-cover blurb. An extract; "his world picture was his word picture and his vocabulary, obscene," — p. 87. Other works by Trocchi include; *My life and loves: fifth volume*. Paris: Olympia Press, 1955. 186 p. (Traveller's companion series; no. 10).; *Cain's book*. New York: Grove Press, 1960. 252 p.; *Young Adam*. London: Heinemann, 1961. 161 p.; *The outsiders*. New York: New American Library of World Literature, 1961. 160 p. (A Signet book).; *School for wives*. North Hollywood : Brandon House, 1967. 207 p. (Originally published: Lengel, Francis. *School for sin*. Paris: Olympia Press, 1955).; *The carnal days of Helen Seferis*. North Hollywood: Brandon House, 1967. 191 p.; *Helen and desire*. North Hollywood: Brandon House, 1967. 208 p.; *Thongs*. North Hollywood: Brandon House, 1967. 191 p.; *White thighs*. North Hollywood: Brandon House, 1967. 208 p.; and *Sappho of Lesbos: the autobiography of a strange woman, translated from the mediaeval Latin*. London: W.H. Allen, 1986 (1st pub. 1960). 220 p. Many of these works were first published by Trocchi under the name of Frances Lengel.

3.9 Raoul Vaneigem. 1934-

140.
Vaneigem, Raoul. Terrorisme ou révolution. In : Coeurderoy, Ernest. [1825-1862]. *Pour la révolution*. Paris: Éditions Champ Libre, 1972. 336 p. (Classiques de la subversion, 2-3) : pp. 7-44.

> Substantial preface by Vaneigem. Also by Vaneigem see; *Adresse aux vivants: sur la mort qui les gouverne et l'opportunité de s'en défaire*. Paris: Seghers, 1990. 261 p.; *Louis Scutenaire*. Paris: Seghers, 1991. 185 p., ill. ISBN 2232103218. (Poétes d'aujourd'hui).; and *Lettre de Staline à ses enfants, enfin réconiliés, de l'Est et de l'Quest*. Levallois-Perret, France: Manya, 1992. 96 p. ISBN 2878960467. (Roman biographique).

141.
[Vaneigem, Raoul] Ratgeb. *De la grève sauvage à l'autogestion généralisée*. Paris: Union générale d'éditions, 1974.

> Translated by Paul Sharkey as; *Contributions to the revolutionary struggle intended to be discussed, corrected and principally put into practice without delay*. London: Bratach Dubh Editions, 1981. 45 p. There was also a second edition; London: Elephant Editions, 1990. 47 p. ISBN 1870133560. (Bratach Dubh Anarchist Pamphlets 7). "The ABC of revolution. A) The object of sabotage and misappropriation, whether practised by the individual or the group, is the unleashing of a wildcat strike. B) Every wildcat strike must develop into a factory occupation. C) Every factory occupied must be appropriated and turned promptly to the service of revolutionaries. D) By choosing delegates (who are subject to instant recall and mandated to collate decisions and to oversee their implementation) the assembled strikers lay the groundwork for a radical reorganisation of society ... into a society of universal selfmanagement." — Ratgeb, p. 30 (original punctuation).

142.
Vaneigem, Raoul. *The revolution of everyday life*. London: Practical Paradise [distributed by Unitary Space Time Publishers], 1975. 292 p.

> Translation by John Fullerton and Paul Sieveking of; *Traité de savoir-vivre à l'usage des jeunes générations*. Paris: Gallimard, 1967. 287 p. (reprinted in 1973 and 1978). A revised edition of this translation was published by; London: Rising Free Collective, 1979. 280 p., ill. Another

translation, "approved by the author" — t.p., by Donald Nicholson-Smith was published in; Seattle, Washington: Left Bank Books and London: Rebel Press, 1983, 216 p., ill. ISBN 0946061017 (UK) and 0939306069 (USA). This last edition includes the 1972 postscript 'A toast to revolutionary workers.' The book is also being serialized in *Anarchy: a journal of desire armed*. The first section of *Traité...* was translated and published as; *Treatise on living for the use of the young generation*. New York: Situationist International, [1970?]. 63 p., ill. The full text was also translated into Spanish as; *Tratado del saber vivir para uso de las jóvenes generaciones*. Barcelona: Anagrama, 1977. 295 p. ISBN 8433913042. (La educación sentimental; 4). A German translation was published as; *Handbuch der Lebenskunst für die Jungen Generationen*. Hamburg: Nautilus, [n.d.]. *Reference from Ohrt [45], p. 335. Translated into Portuguese by José Carlos Marques as; *A arte de viver para a geraçänova*. Porto: Afrontamento, 1975. 297 p. (O saco de Lacraus; 3). There is also said to have been an edition of the translation of Vaneigem's 'Banalitiés de Base' published as; *The totality for kids*. York: Alternative Prospectus, 1979. There was also a translation of this by Christopher Gray and Philippe Vissac published by Christopher Gray some time around 1964.

143.
[Vaneigem, Raoul] Jules François Dupuis. *Histoire désinvolte du surréalisme*. Nonville: Éditions Paul Vermont, 1977. 164 p. (Collection Le Rappel au désordre).

Also published by; Paris: Instant, 1988. 164 p. ISBN 2869291264. Translated into Italian as; *Controstoria del surrealismo*. Roma: Arcana Editrice, 1978. 126 p. ISBN 8885008011. (Situazioni; 28). Translation by Rodolfo Demartinis. "Everywhere Surrealism appears in recuperated forms: commodities, works of art, publicity techniques, the language of power, a model of alienated imagination, objects of devotion, and cultural accessories" — J-F. Dupois [Vaneigem] in; Henri Béhar and Michel Carassou, (eds.). Le *Surréalisme: textes and débats*. Paris: Librairie Générale Française, 1984, p. 69. *Reference from Plant [47], p. 78.

144.
Vaneigem, Raoul. *Le livre des plaisirs*. Paris: Encre, 1979. 208 p. ISBN 2864180383. (L'Atelier du possible).

Translated by John Fullerton as; *The book of pleasures*. London: Pending Press, 1983. 105 p. ISBN 0904665038. A slightly disappointing follow-up to *The revolution of everyday life*. "Doing exactly what you feel like is pleasure's greatest weapon, connecting individual acts with collective practice; we all do it. If rejecting survival made the 1968 movement, taking hold of life will open the era of universal self-management." — Vaneigem, backcover. Excerpts published as; Vaneigem, Raoul. *Excerpts from the book of pleasures* [Junction City, Kansas: Garrett Michael O'Hara, August 11, 1984, 8 p., ill., edition 100]?. "A hostile review of Ratgeb and Book of pleasures" by; Black, Bob. Quit while you're ahead. *Social Anarchism*. 4 (7 [or 1]), 1984, pp. 26-30. This was also reprinted in *Dharma Combat*. (11), 1991, p. 7. *References from Bob Black correspondence.

145.
Vaneigem, Raoul. *Le mouvement du Libre-Espiri: généralitiés et témoignages sur les affleurements de la vie à la surface du Moyen Age, de la Renaissance et, incidemment, de notre époque*. Paris: Éditions Ramsay, 1986. 263 p. ISBN 2859565191.

On the Brethren of the Free Spirit and other medieval sects. Soon to be published as; *Movement of the Free Spirit: generalities about the testimony of the outcrops of life in the surface of the Middle Ages, the Renaissance, and, incidentally, our epoch: the perspective of the market and the perspective of life*. New York: Zone Books, 1993. ISBN 0942299701. Translated by Ian Patterson.

3.10 René Viénet. 1944-

146.
Viénet, René and Cohen, Gerard. *La dialectique peut-elle casser des briques*. Produced by L'Oiseau de Minerve. (1973; colour, 90 minutes.)

An edition (VHS) with English subtitles translated as *Can dialectics break bricks?* was reported to be available from Drift Distribution, 219 E. 2nd Street #5E, New York, NY 10009 in; *Anarchy: a journal of desire armed*. 13 (1), 1993, p. 18. The film is described by Levin as; "... an amusing example of the use of détournement to rewrite or re-function ... an otherwise highly compromised product of the culture industry. This full length 35mm color film by Doo Kwang Gee is a transformation ... of a classic Hong Kong Kung-Fu film ... into a didactic suspense narrative illustrating the conflict between the proletariat and the bureaucrats! ... Another Chinese film détourned by Inez Tan and René Viénet through the addition of French subtitles, *Du sang chez les Taoists* (1971; colour, 80 min.), seems to be currently unavailable. Very little information is available concerning the three further films that Viénet and his collaborators are supposed to have détourned: *Une petite culotte pour l'été, Une soutanne n'a pas de braguette,* and *L'aubergine est farcie."* — Levin, p. 111 in Sussman [57].

147.
Viénet, René. *Enragés and Situationists in the Occupation movement, France, May '68.* New York; London: Autonomedia; Rebel Press, 1992. 158 p., ill. ISBN 0936756799 (US) & 094606105X (UK).

First published as; *Enragés et situationnistes dans le mouvement des occupations.* Paris: Gallimard, 1968. 316 p., ill. (Collection Témoins). Also published as a photocopied transcript translated by Loren Goldner and Paul Sieveking as; *Enragés and Situationists in the Occupation Movement, France, May-June 1968.* Heslington, York: Tiger Papers, [1972?]. 24 p., ill. This or a similar translation by Loren Goldner was also published in Belgium; [Brussels: s.n., 1968] 42 p. *Reference from OCLC. The book was also translated into Spanish as; *Enragés, y situacionistas en el movimiento de las ocupaciones.* Madrid: Castellote Editor, 1978. 202 p., ill. ISBN 847259095X. Viénet's book documents the role played by two of the most influential groups involved in the May '68 uprisings. An interesting aspect of the book is its documentation of a time of great revolutionary fervour and the development of a political use of graffiti, telegrams, songs, altered comics, posters and poetry. The historical accuracy may be shaky but as a document of Situationist lore it ranks alongside Debord's [91] and Vaneigem's [142] key publications. See also; Marbot, Bernard, and Viénet, René. *Notes sur quelques photographies de la Chine au XIXe siécle: à l'occasion de l'exposition "La Chine entre le collodion humide & le gélatinobromure".* Paris: Centre de publication Asie orientale, 1978. 59 p., ill. (Bibliothéque asiatique; 43).

3.11 Gil J Wolman. 1929-

148.

Wolman, Gil J. *Résumé des chapitres précédents*. Paris: Spiess, 1981.

"Artistic autobiography by détournement: works, writings, reviews; includes numerous examples of scotch art." — *Reference from Marcus [42], p. 462. Also by Wolman; Wolman, Gil J. (as Joseph Wolman) *Durhing, Durhing*. Paris, September, 1979. "... Wolman published a thick tabloid he called *Durhing Durhing*. On each of the sixty-four pages are fifty-four tightly cropped faces, more than three thousand in all: commonplace images of sitting politicians, dead statesmen, movie stars ... every variety of celebrity." Marcus [42], p. 366.

149.

Wolman, Gil J. Wolman. *L'Oeil*. (Lausanne, Switzerland), (351), October 1984, p. 77, ill.

Very short notice of Wolman's exhibition at the Galerie Nane Stern, 25, avenue de Tourville, 75007 Paris. "Jusqu'au 3 novembre. Du 20 au 28 octobre: FIAC au Grand Palais. [1984]" Also mentions *Vivre et Mourir précédé* de *Introduction et séparation du mot*. Which may refer to; Wolman, J. *Vivre et Mourir*. Paris: Spiess et N. Stern, 1984. Also by Wolman; Ralentissez les cadences, mégapneume. In: Dufrêne, François, (ed.) *L'Autonomatopek 1*. Opus International, 1973. *Reference from Marcus [42], p. 453.

3.12 Maurice Wyckaert. 1923-

150.

Richir, Marc. *L'orée du monde: Maurice Wyckaert*. [The edge of the world]. *Esprit* (France), (2), 1986, p. 52-60, ill.

"Maurice Wyckaert, né à Bruxelles en 1923, a été lié au groupe Cobra, en particulier à Asger Jorn et Christian Dotremont. Il a participé à la fondation et aux débuts du mouvement situationniste. Nombreuses expositions en Belgique, en Italie (Venise, Milan), en Allemagne (Munich), aux Pays-Bas (Eindhoven) et à Paris (Galerie Ariel). Participation à de nombreuses biennales et autres manifestations de groupe. Oeuvres dans les musées d'Anvers, Gand, Bruxelles, Silkeborg, Vienne, Lausanne, Helsinki, Sao Paulo, Bochum,

Pittsburgh... Nous remercions la revue *La part de l'oeil* (Bruxelles), d'avoir bien voulu nous autoriser à reproduire de larges extraits de cet article, publié dans son numéro de mars 1985." — Notes on the artist. Also on Wyckaert see; *Maurice Wyckaert*. Bergamo: Galleria Lorenzelli, 1972. [49] p., ill. With essays by Max Loreau and Michel Seuphor.; *Wyckaert*. Antwerpen: Lens Fine Art, [1974]. [39] p., ill. Catalogue of an exhibition held Nov. 21, 1974 — Jan. 11, 1975.; Loreau, Max. *Wyckaert*. [S.l.: s.n.], 1975. [32] p., ill. Text in English and Portuguese for the XIII Bienal Sao Paulo, 1975.; and Vree, Freddy de. ... [et al.]. *Wyckaert*. Antwerpen: Lanno/Fonds Mercator, 1986. 222 p., ill. ISBN 9020913883.

AMERICAN PRO-SITUS & MILIEU

151.
Against Sleep and Nightmare. 1- . Oakland: A.S.A.N., [1988?-].
Contents of number two include; 'Hatred and violence', 'The spectacle's critique of the spectacle', 'The project of supersession' and 'The crisis of capital'. A.S.A.N. PO Box 3305 Oakland CA 94609. Periodical published yearly. "A.S.A.N. is part of the debate on strategy among a very small group of revolutionaries. Within this milieu, there are those who call themselves 'ultra-leftist', 'council communist', 'autonomist', 'situationist-influenced', 'class-war anarchist', or 'left communist.'" — Editorial, from issue number 4. They also published; *The Punishers*. Oakland: Against Sleep and Nightmare, [n.d.]. 12 p., Short text, with illustrations from comics, concerning drugs.

152.
Anon. Drifting with the Situationist International. *Anarchy: a journal of desire armed.* (21), Summer 1991, pp. 20-21, ill.
A plain beginners guide to the S.I. "...their theory and praxis of the situation, dérive and détournement, constitute an imaginative advance in political tactics suited to that society. Their work both desires and requires further experimentation and development." — p. 21. Reprinted from Schiz-flux. *Smut* (*Smile*) (5), [1991?], pp. 24-26. This particular edition of the 'Magazine of multiple origins' is subtitled 'Journal of illicit sex and hardcore exposure: 4th Reich report and child sexuality.'

153.
Black, Bob. The realization and suppression of Situationism. *Anarchy: a journal of desire armed.* (29), Summer 1991, pp. 18-19.
Discussion of Situationist 'fall-out' culminating in the travelling show. "The S.I. was forever discovering *unconscious* situationism in the conduct of Watts rioters, juvenile delinquents, Katangan rebels and even Berkeley students. ... As much is implicitly situationist — and more is explicitly situationist — in the marginals milieu of 1991 as in the punk milieu of the mid-70's, but the mortician's client first has to be dead. Situationism is dead. Long live Situationism!"- Black,

p. 19. Edited version first appeared in; *Artpaper*. 9 (6), February 1990, pp. 14-15, ill. Also by Bob Black; What is "Situationism?" *Research*. (2), 1981, p. 29. "At this late date, that which is alive in situationism most often makes itself felt in the activity of intransigents who are indifferent to the 'situationist' label or even disclaim it." — Black, pp. 29. For more Black see; Black, Bob. *The baby and the bathwater, or post-partum repression: the unspeakable truth about Processed World*. 1-1/2th ed. Berkeley: Slobboviated Press, 1985. 164 p., ill.; Black, Bob. *The abolition of work and other essays*. Port Townsend, Washington: Loompanics, [1986]. 159 p. ISBN 0915179415; and Black, Bob and Parfrey, Adam. *Rants and incendiary tracts: voices of desperate illumination, 1558 to the present*. New York: Amok Press and Port Townsend: Loompanics, 1989. 219 p. ISBN. 0941693031. This last item includes 'Formulary for a new urbanism' by Ivan Chtcheglov (pp. 131-136) and the anonymous 'Situationist Liberation Front' an early seventies poster (pp. 165-166).

154.

Bloch, Nadine. *All things considered*, 1976. Berkeley: Gina Rosenberg, 1976. 11 p.

Pamphlet printed on blue paper. A translation of *Compte-rendu, 1976* by Gina Rosenberg with assistance from the author. "In September 1973 I participated in the formation of the Center for Research on the Social Question from which I resigned in December 1975. At that time, all things considered, I definitely had to acknowledge my personal failure during those two years, which can be summed up as follows: I did not have during that period any individual theoretico-practical activity." — Bloch, p. 1.

155.

Brook, J[ames]. Situationism: notes toward a testament in transit... *Research*. (1), [1980], p. 28.

A short text by J. Brook. "The situationists confused art with its social function. To paint, to write, to compose, to film, is not automatically to shore up an ideology of aestheticism or the art market. And not to commit art is no proof against aestheticism — there is a situationist aesthetic trademarking their pamphlets, agit-prop cartoons, vocabulary, author-itarian posing." — Brook.

156.

Brown, Bill, ed. *Not Bored!* (PO Box 3421, Wayland Sq., Providence, RI 02906). 1983- , 1-

"*Not Bored!* was first published in Ann Arbor, Michigan, in July 1983 as an outlet for short articles on music that freelance writer and weekly columnist Bill Brown (then 24) couldn't publish in *The Ann Arbor News* because of their political content. *Not Bored!*'s purpose and focus shifted with the second issue (January 1984) as a result of Brown's reading first Greil Marcus' review [40] of the *Situationist International anthology* [35] and then the *Anthology* itself. Now up to its 21st issue (July 1992), *Not Bored!* has remained Situationist inspired since then... "- Bill Brown statement; In : Perkins, Stephen *Zine show.* Iowa : The author, 1992: p. 11.

157.

Bureau of Control. *State of the Art: for today's artist.* [Texas: Bureau of Control], 1990. 40 p., ill.

Small photocopied booklet, illustrated on cover with Marcel Duchamp's 'Urinal' and inside with 'survivalist' imagery. Contains a radical critique of art as commodity. "The avant-garde artist is an unpaid researcher for the mainstream. He or she explores the cultural wilderness. If it looks exploitable, along comes the cops, priests, settlers and banks. The artist is crowded out and must go exploring again." — anon, [Bureau of Control]. Real art is said to occur when there is no distinction between the artist and the audience.

158.

Capitalist Crisis Studies. *Beyond the nation-state, the world market, and blind development: toward a program-of-transition to Socialism.* Berkeley: CCS, March 1977. [40] p.

Also includes 'Socialist programatics: the method of discovery'. "For presentation to the West Coast Regional Conference to build the Nationwide Unemployed League October 4th and 5th, 1975. CCS P.O. Box 754, Berkeley, California 94701." — CCS, p. [40].

159.

Carlsson, Chris and Leger, Mark (eds). *Bad attitude: the Processed World anthology.* London: Verso, 1990. 281 p., ill. ISBN 0860912841.

A large format anthology with many excellent graphics and much anti-work ranting. "*Processed World*'s founders came out of the ultra-left fringe politics, self-schooled in the classic anarchists, the anti-bolshevik communists of the 'teens and the 'twenties, and — especially — the work of the Situationist International (SI) in the 'fifties and 'sixties." — Carlsson and Adam Cornford, p. 13. Other texts by Adam Cornford include; *Reader's orgasm.* East Lansing, Michigan: *The Spectacle,* 1976. [28] p., ill.; and *Animations.* San Francisco: City Lights Books, 1988. 99 p. ISBN 0872862089. (Pocket poets series; no. 45).

160.

Carrion, Tita ... [et al.]. *Notice concerning the reigning society and those who contest it.* Berkeley: [s.n.], Nov. 1974, 1 sheet folded, printed one side.

Brown text on cream paper. The other contributors were Robert Cooperstein, Issac Cronin, Dan Hammer, Ken Knabb, Gina Rosenberg, and Chris Shutes. Reprinted in *Implications* pp. 45-46. "An intentionally provocative manifesto on revolutionary organization and the relations between the signers. There was a falling out among the latter in 1977." — Ken Knabb, correspondence, 1991.

161.

Chasse, Robert. *The power of negative thinking or Robin Hood rides again.* New York: The Council for the Liberation of Daily Life, April, 1968. 41 p., ill.

Address given as: The Council for the Liberation of Daily Life, Box 666, Stuyvesant Station, New York, N.Y., 10009. "The consciousness of liberation passes through the liberation of consciousness" — Chasse, contents page. Chasse's examination paper for his entry into the S.I. "The American section's main publication... a critique of the new left actually published shortly before Chasse joined the S.I." — Knabb [35], p. 379. The one and only issue of the American's review has been reprinted as: *Situationist International: review of the American Section of the S.I. Number 1 - June 1969.* Portland, Ore.: Extreme Press, 1993. 46 p.

162.
[Chasse, Robert and Elwell, Bruce]. *A field study in the dwindling force of cognition, where it is least expected: a critique of the Situationist International as a revolutionary organization.* [New York]: [The authors], Feb-Mar. 1970. 46 p.

Contents: 'The seriousness of what is not serious', 'Here we rose to dance', 'To the formation of a section', 'The American section to the 8th conference', 'The 8th conference' [Venice], 'The Fall crisis', 'The logic of falsification', and an appendix containing the 'Provisional statutes', 'Participation in the S.I.', 'Organization of national sections', and 'Coordination between sections'. "After their resignation and exclusion in December 1969, Chasse and Elwell produced an extensive critical history of the American section, *A field study ...* contesting the manner of their exclusion." — Knabb [35], p. 379.

163.
Chernyi, Lev. The situationists and beyond. *Anarchy: a journal of desire armed.* (29), Summer 1991, pp. 14-15.

Introduction to a special feature on the situationists, which denounces their Marxist leanings and celebrates their more anarchist tendencies. "The tension between these two sides of their theory and practice permeates their legacy, leaving it for anarchists to disentangle the rotting threads of Marxist ideology from the rest of the living body of libertarian theory." — Chernyi, p. 14.

164.
Collective Inventions. *Defence mechanisms.* San Jose, CA.: Collective Inventions, April, 15th 1980. [13] p. ill.

Also by the group; Collective Inventions. *Consumer's guide to the Jam.* San Jose, CA.: Collective Inventions, Memorial Day, 1982, 3 p. ill.; and Collective Inventions. *Poland 1982.* San Jose, CA.: Collective Inventions, Jan. 10th, 1982. "In format [this] is a pamphlet unfolding into a single large sheet, about 33"x23", illustrated." — *References from Bob Black correspondence.

165.
Cooperstein, Robert. *Some notes on the reproduction of human capital.* Berkeley: Robert Cooperstein, April, 1974. 15 p., ill.

"The following remarks will pertain for the most part to the child's immediate position within the familial situation, and not to his more extensive relation with the spectacle in its entirety." — Cooperstein, inside front cover. A poster was also produced for this with similar 'colour in' cartoons.

166.

Cooperstein, Robert. *The crisis of the gross national spectacle*. Berkeley: Robert Cooperstein, [Jan. 1976]. 13 p.

Also of related interest is; Anon. [satirically attributed to "Robert 'Bobby' Cooperstein"] Editorial: the role of plastics in the present struggle. *Fli-back: A journal of cheap shots*. Detroit, Michigan, Feb. 1976, pp. 37 -39. "One shot from some Fifth Estate people, this text satirizing the San Francisco pro-situs." — *Reference from Bob Black correspondence.

167.

Create Situations. *The beginning of an epoch*. New York: Create Situations, [1971?]. 47 p., ill.

Title on cover *The poor and the super-poor*. "The following texts were first published together in number 11 (Oct. 1967) of the Internationale Situationiste [sic]." — Inside front cover. Translations of 'Contributions serving to rectify the opinion of the public concerning the revolution in underdeveloped countries', 'The explosion point of ideology in China', and' Two local wars' by 'A.C.' [Adam Cornford] and 'T.V.' [Tony Verlaan].

168.

Cronin, Issac [1948-] and Seltzer, Terrel. *Call it sleep*. London: B.M. Combustion, 1983, 22 p., ill.

Transcript of videotape (42 mins.) written and directed by the above and edited by Don Ahrens. Camera, Don Ahrens, Kathleen Beeler; sound, Robert Cooperstein, David Floeter, Ian Turner; narration, Bruce Parry. The pamphlet is divided into a four part analysis of: 'The spectacle', 'Bolshevism', 'The cadre', and 'The new revolt'. "Call it sleep is the first visual work produced in the United States which makes use of the situationist technique of détournement — the devaluation and reuse of present and past cultural production to form a superior theoretical and practical unity." — Backcover. Also by Cronin; Cronin, Issac and Hammer, Dan. *Cleveland Indian war*. San Francisco: Issac Cronin, July 1974. Leaflet; Cronin, Issac. *Critique of* *counterfeitism.* San Francisco: Issac Cronin, [1975?]. [8] p.; and Cronin, Issac. *San Francisco Chronicle.* Jan. 1975. Self published wall poster. *Reference from Bob Black correspondence. Also by Cronin; *Champagne!* New York: Long Shadow Books, 1984. 96 p.; and *The international squid cookbook.* Berkeley, CA.: Aris Books, 1981. 96 p., ill.

169.
Denevert, Daniel. *Theory of misery/misery of theory: report on the new conditions of revolutionary theory.* Paris: Centre de Recherche sur la Question Sociale, 1974. 16 p.

Translated by Robert Cooperstein, Dan Hammer and Ken Knabb. Also included extracts from 'For the intelligence of some aspects of the moment' and 'Declaration concerning the Center for Research on the Social Question' [C.R.S.Q.]. First published in France in 1973. "Even if a *constituted* situationist theory had never existed as a possible source of inspiration, the system of commodity consumption implicitly contains its *own situationism.*" —Denevert. "The organized theoretical effort — the most advanced since Marx — carried out by the members of the Situationist International has not only burned itself out but even seems to want to be content with a place among the curiosities in the museum of revolutionary history." — Denevert, p. 1. The C.R.Q.S consisted of Françoise Bloch, Jeanne Charles [Françoise Denevert?], Joël Cornuault, and Daniel Denevert.

170.
[Denevert, Françoise?], Charles, Jeanne. *Arms and the Woman.* Berkeley: Bureau of Public Secrets, 1974. 4 p.

Article on women and the Situationist milieu translated by Ken Knabb.

171.
Ex-For Ourselves. *Whatever happened to 'For Ourselves'?* [Berkeley]: [Capitalist Crisis Studies], [n.d.]. 41 p. ill.

Collection of statements on the dissolution of the group. Contents: 'J's statement; F.O. — a history and a psychological critique', 'Gerard's statement: For Ourselves is gone, long live the proletariat For Itself', 'Jenny Diver's statement: the no growth political economy of F.O.', 'Feanor's statement: no more For Ourselves but still for ourselves', 'Louis Michaelson's statement: F.O.: elements for a self-critique',

'Charles Lutwidge's statement; illustrations of Charles Lutwidge's neighbours'. "In February 1974 we published our preamble or founding statement" — Michaelson. Note: Rumours exist that Louis Michaelson is actually Adam Cornford.

172.
Fleming, Jim and Wilson, Peter Lamborn, (eds.). *Semiotext [e] U.S.A.* (13). New York: Autonomedia, 1987. 352 p., ill. ISSN 009395779.

A massive anthology of the American 'marginals' scene. A good introduction to many groups that, although not specifically Situationist, have appropriated and used some of the best bits. Contents include: 'The abolition of work' by Bob Black; 'Theses on Groucho Marx' by the Last International; 'Anarchist-Marxism' by Red & Black Action from *Point-Blank* (4); and a selection from the excellent *Anarchy Comics* which often used the détourned comic technique. At the back of the book you will find a 'Directory of Contributors' with addresses.

173.
For Ourselves. *The right to be greedy: theses on the practical necessity of demanding everything*. Berkeley: For Ourselves, Council for Generalized Self-management, Feb. 1974. [56] p.

Also published as; *The right to be greedy: a situationist synthesis of communism and Stirnerite egoism*. [S.l.]: Revisionist Press, Aug. 1984. ISBN 0877006504. Published most recently as; *The right to be greedy*. Port Townsend, Washington: Loompanics Unlimited, [1986]. Unpaginated [126 theses]. ISBN 0915179350. This edition includes an appendix 'Preamble to the founding agreements of For Ourselves, Council for Generalized Self-management'. Preface and reading list by Bob Black. In his preface Black describes the roots of the book's 'Marxism-Stirnerism'. "In the early 1970's, 'pro-situ' groups (as they are known) formed in Britain, in New York City and especially in the San Francisco Bay Area. One of these groups, Negation, reformed as For Ourselves around 1973, and by the following Mayday produced the present text. For Ourselves was particularly beholden to the situationist Raoul Vaneigem whose celebration of the 'radical subjectivity' of 'masters without slaves' figures prominently in the theory espoused in *The right to be greedy*. All too soon the group collapsed, some of its members regressing into Marxism from which they had never really escaped." — Black. In the reading list at the back of the book Black states that the principal author of *The right to be greedy* was Bruce Gardner and that Tom Ward was a member of the group. Other For Ourselves material includes; For Ourselves. *In Portugal: capital confronts the world proletariat.* Berkeley: For Ourselves, 1974. ; [For Ourselves]. *The minimum definition of intelligence — theses on the construction of one's own self theory.* London: Spectacular Times, 1985. *References from Barry Pateman correspondence.

174.
Friends of the Jura Federation. *Time recaptured: self-management and the LIP occupation.* Berkeley: Point-Blank!, 1973. [11] p., ill.
 Pamphlet on the Lip watch factory occupation by 1300 workers in 1973. "In organizing their activities by themselves, the Lip workers have affirmed their autonomy against the combined machinery of capitalism, the French Left, and the national trade unions." — Friends of the Jura Federation, p. [1]. "Since the implication of the Lip occupations concern everyone, we will distribute this text as widely as possible, in order to contribute to further world-wide agitation and to the development of a situationist revolution." — Point-Blank!, back cover.

175.
Great Atlantic Radio Conspiracy. *For a Situationist Revolution/Movement for a New Society.* 1977 and 1977. GARC. 60 min cassette.
 "Although quite different, both of these groups are examples of contemporary anarchism. The first [the S.I.] was perhaps one of the most exciting and theoretically fascinating of our time, playing an important role in France 1968. M.N.S. [Movement for a New Society] is a non-violent, decentralised federation of living and working groups in American cities. The tactics and strategies of each group are discussed." *Reference from *AK Distribution 1993 catalogue* [222], p. 57. " [Cassettes] produced by the Great Atlantic Radio Conspiracy (GARC) are a series of different half hour radio shows that they broadcast regularly, and usually feature a mixture of comment, interviews, some music etc. There are two GARC shows per cassette. Dates shown are of broadcast." — p. 56.

176.
Greenberg, Jeffrey, (ed). Against the spectacle: private and inter-personal experiment, social and political activity. *The Act.* 2 (1), 1990. 100 p., ill. ISSN 08856702.

Special issue including essays by Gran Fury, Allan Kaprow and Carolee Schneemann. Very little to do with the Debordian concept of the spectacle except the essay 'Skeptical of the Spectacle' by Suzanne Lacy, pp. 36-42.

177.
Hahne, Ron, and Morea, Ben. *Black Mask and the Motherfuckers: the incomplete works of Ron Hahne, Ben Morca and the Black Mask Group.* London: Unpopular Books and Sabotage Editions, 1993. 144 p., ill. ISBN 1873176708.

An important anthology that helps to reset the balance of influence that was active in the late sixties. The Motherfuckers were in contact with the London based Heatwave group (actually contributing to the English section's expulsion from the S.I.) which in turn became King Mob. The book consists of reprints of the Black Mask 'newsletter', leaflets, the *Motherfucker* magazine and an extensive report on a press conference. "Black Mask grasped almost intuitively the crux of the 1910-25 art crisis; that the content of modern art, the vision of a totally created world stemming from the first romantics, was potentially the most vitriolic attack on bourgeois civilisation ever made; while, on the contrary, its form strait-jacketed it within a purely reactionary role. Taken literally it is dynamite. Taken culturally it is one of the system's main supports." King Mob, quoted on the back cover. Those connected with the group include Tony Verlaan, Dan Georgakas and Dave and Stuart Wise. Georgakas has amongst other things co-edited; *The Encyclopedia of the American Left.* London: St. James, 1990. [930] p., ill. ISBN 1558621210.; and authored *Left face: a source book of radical magazines, presses, and collectives actively involved in the arts.* New York: Cineaste and Smyrna Press, 1978. 16 p. ISBN 0918266084. For information on another, unrelated underground group, the Weather Underground Organisation see; *Outlaws of Amerika: communiques from the Weather Underground.* New York: Liberated Guardian, [1971]. 48 p., ill. "This pamphlet was prepared by the Liberated Guardian Collective and other friends of the Weather Underground. Text of most of the communiques from documents sent to The Liberated Guardian, others from the YIPPIES, and the Berkeley tribe and other papers." The Weather Underground published a quarterly periodical, Spring 1975- , called *Osawatomie*.

178.

Horelick, Jon. (ed.). *Diversion 1*. New York: Diversion, June 1973, 56 p., ill. Periodical in the style of *Internationale situationniste*. Includes the following: 'The poverty of ecology', 'News of disalienation', 'Twilight of the idle', [translation of] 'Notice to the civilized' [from *I.S.* (12)], and 'The practice of the truth: the crisis of the Situationist International'.

179.

Horelick, Jon. *Beyond the crisis of abstraction and the abstract break with the crisis: the S.I.* New York: Diversion, 1974.

One A4 sheet printed both sides with 14 theses. "Situationism belongs, for the most part, to the student in his romance with revolutionary extremism ... The appearance of *Diversion* did not bear the intention of either reviving a situationist theory or getting rid of one. It was simply preoccupied with the real use for this theory in locating the route of revolutionary praxis, the noose of unified opposition which tightens around the neck of the old world as words and deeds become one." — Horelick. Also possibly by Horelick and Tony Verlaan see; Council for the Eruption of the Marvellous. *On wielding the subversive scalpel*. [S.l.]: [s.n.], 1970. 16 p., ill. *Reference from Bob Black correspondence.

180.

Igor, Boy. *And yet it moves: the realization and suppression of science and technology*. New York: Zamisdat Press, 1985. 121 p., ill. ISBN 0934727007.

"Of all the spectacles science is the least attacked. In a society where power is everywhere diffused and everywhere attacked, the appeal to science has become a final authority." — Igor, p. 9.

181.

Italy: Autonomia: post political politics. *Semiotext[e]*. 3 (3), 1980. 316 p. ISSN 009395779. (Intervention series 1).

Described by Bob Black in his 'Reading list' [173] as a; "Book-length anthology on the theory and practice of 'autonomist' resistance in

Italy, with scathing if brief attacks on the Red Brigades as creatures of the Italian Government by the situationists Debord and Sanguinetti." — Black.

182.
Jacobs, David and Winks, Christopher. *At dusk: the Situationist movement in historical perspective.* Berkeley: Perspectives, [Aug] 1975. 97 p.

A key and extensive text from the American pro-situ scene. Contains an extensive critique of Situationist concepts benefiting very much with the advantage of hindsight. Many of its perspectives have turned up in other subsequent critiques of the group.

183.
Klein, Stephanie (aka Gidget Digit). *Bizarro Processed World: special Gidget am fired!* Menlo Park, CA.: [The author], Sept. 9, 1986. 31 p., ill.

"This is not a review of *Processed World*. It is a return of the repressed. I was a member of *Processed World* in 1981, and I was fired, so to speak, from the PW collective for having a 'bad attitude' about the magazine ... I've spent the last four years remaining silent on the matter, even during the several subsequent controversies that sprang up between *PW* and its critics." — Klein, p. 1. A revealing history and review of the relationship between the Bay Area milieu and *Processed World*.

184.
Knabb, Ken. *Remarks on Contradiction and its failure.* Berkeley: Bureau of Public Secrets, March 1973. 16 p.

"A collection of almost all of the publications of Contradiction, '1044' and the C.E.M. is filed under 'Bureau of Public Secrets' in Berkeley ('Boss Files', Reference Room, Berkeley Public Library, Shattuck and Kittredge) and Amsterdam (Anarchism Department, International Institute of Social History, Herengracht 262-266)." — Knabb. "It was primarily a critique, a correction of Contradiction's orientation toward the movement (and first of all of its very notion of such a unified 'movement'), of the way we went about a certain task." — Knabb, p. 29 in *Bureau of Public Secrets 1*. Translated by Daniel Denevert as; *Remarques sur le groupe Contradiction et son échec.* published by C.R.Q.S. in April 1974.

185.

Knabb, Ken. *Double reflection: preface to a phenomenology of the subjective aspect of practical-critical activity*. Berkeley: Bureau of Public Secrets, May 1974. 16 p.
> Yellow covered pamphlet. "On the subjective/psychological aspects of situationist-type radical activity."- Knabb, publicity material. "'Sooner or later the S.I. must define itself as therapeutic' — *I.S.* (8), 1963. Each time an individual rediscovers revolt he remembers his previous experiences of it, which all come back to him like a sudden memory of childhood." — Knabb, p. 1. Translated into French with the aid of Joël Cornuault as *Double-Réflection*, 1974 and published by the C.R.Q.S. "In November 1974 *Double-Reflection* was reprinted by Spontaneous Combustion." — Knabb, p. 33, in *Bureau of Public Secrets 1*.

186.

Knabb, Ken. ed. *Bureau prehistory*. Berkeley: Bureau of Public Secrets, 1975. [86] p., ill.
> "Xerox collection of publications by three San Francisco — Berkeley situationist groups. 'The Council for the Eruption of the Marvellous', '1044', and 'Contradiction' (1970-72). Includes comics, leaflets, pamphlets, 'Great moments in the void' trading cards, and unpublished articles on the American radical movement and counter-culture. 1973"— Ken Knabb correspondence. "Duplicated here, in an edition of 30 copies, all the texts included in the Bureau of Public Secrets 'Prehistory' collection in Amsterdam, Berkeley and New York, except for those which are merely reprints from the S.I. — K.K., June 1975." *Reference from OCLC.

187.

Knabb, Ken. *The blind men und the elephant*. Berkeley: Bureau of Public Secrets, 1975.
> "Large poster with amusingly diverse quotations about the Situationist International, ranging from delirious hostility to confused approval. Later incorporated as appendix of the *Situationist International anthology*." — Knabb, correspondence. Included here is a selected list of references from *The blind men and the elephant* not elsewhere listed in this bibliography; *Anarchy* (7), Winter 1972 ; *Workers' councils and the economics of a self-managed society*. Solidarity (England), March 1972 ; Richard Johnson, *The French Communist*

party versus the students, 1972 ; *New Morning,* February 1973 ; Bruce Brown, *Marx, Freud and the critique of everyday life,* 1973 ; Bernard E. Brown, *Protest in Paris: anatomy of a revolt.* [General Learning Press], 1974 ; *Le Nouvel Observateur,* 29 April 1974 ; *Le Monde,* 9 May 1974 ; *New Solidarity* (paper of the National Caucus of Labor Committees), 28 August and 6 September 1974 (which alleges the S.I. was created by the C.I.A. in 1957) ; *World Revolution,* (3), April 1975 ; David Widgery, *The left in Britain: 1956-68,* 1976 ; Heathcote Williams in *International Times,* Autumn, 1977 ; *Melody Maker,* June 1979 ; Stuart Christie, *The Christie file,* 1980.

188.
Knabb, Ken, (ed.). *Bureau of Public Secrets 1.* Berkeley: Bureau of Public Secrets, January 1976. 40 p., ill.

Only one issue published. Contents; 'Arms and the woman' by Jeanne Charles [pseud. of Françoise Denevert], 'Notes toward a situationist manifesto' by Jeanne Charles and Daniel Denevert (both of these were first published as 'Notes pour une manifeste situationniste' and 'La critique ad mulierem' in *Chronique des secrets publics,* volume 1, June 1975); 'From 'End of science'' by Jean-Louis Moinet (translation of the first thesis of *Fin de la science,* 1974); and 'The society of situationism', 'Affective détournement: a case study' and 'A short guide to the Anglo-American situationist image' all by Knabb.

189.
Knabb, Ken. *The realization and suppression of religion.* Berkeley: Bureau of Public Secrets, March 1977. 15 p.

"Pamphlet on the relation of religion and revolution, with a critique of the Situationists' attitude toward religion. Appendix on anarchist poet-critic Kenneth Rexroth."- Knabb, correspondence. "Developing out of the perspective that to be superseded, art must be both realized and suppressed, situationist theory failed to see that an analogous position was called for regarding religion." — Knabb, p. 1.

190.
Knabb, Ken. *To members of the Tokyo 'Libertaire' group.* Berkeley: Bureau of Public Secrets, 1977.

Critical 'open letter' reprinted with responses in the group's journal *Libertaire.*

191.
Knabb, Ken. *A radical group in Hong Kong*. Berkeley: Bureau of Public Secrets, 1978. 2 p.

"Appreciation and critique of the libertarian group that published *Minus*. Partially reprinted in the Canadian edition of the group's *China: the revolution is dead, long live the revolution*. [Montreal: Black Rose Books, 1977. xvi, 247 p. ISBN 0919618375]" — Knabb, correspondence. See also; Brendal, C. Situationist International: the explosion point of ideology in China. In: *The revolution is dead, long live the revolution; readings on the great proletarian cultural revolution from an ultra-left perspective*. Hong Kong: The 70's, 1976. v, 291p. *Reference from OCLC.

192.
Knabb, Ken. *The opening in Iran*. Berkeley: Bureau of Public Secrets, 1979.

"Poster on the uprising against the Shah. 1979. Translated into French and Greek." — *Reference from Knabb, correspondence.

193.
Knabb, Ken. *The relevance of Rexroth*. Berkeley: Bureau of Public Secrets, 1990. 88 p. ISBN 0939682002.

Book length critique of Kenneth Rexroth. "Even those avant-garde tendencies that have sought to overcome the spectacle aspect of art by encouraging audience participation (in Happenings for example) do so within limitations of space and time that turn such participation into a farce." — Knabb, p. 73.

194.
[Knabb, Ken] Bureau of Public Secrets. *The war and the spectacle*. Berkeley: Bureau of Public Secrets, April 1991. 4 p.

This was also reprinted in; *Anarchy: a journal of desire armed*. (20), Summer 1991, pp. 16-17. "The orchestration of the Gulf war was a glaring expression of what the situationists call the spectacle — the development of modern society to the point where images dominate life. ... alternative media have generally reproduced the dominant spectacle-spectator relation. The point is to undermine it — to challenge the conditioning that makes people susceptible to media manipulation in the first place." — Knabb. Leaflet on the gulf war and the media. "Over 10,000 copies distributed. Widely reprinted, translated into French and Japanese." — Knabb, correspondence.

195.
Lutwidge, Charles. *A modest proposal for how the bad days will end.* [Palo Alto, CA.: Reinvention of Everyday Life, 1975]. 6 p., ill.
    2nd. printing published by; Aberdeen: Social Revolution, 1978. 3rd printing by; [Rising Free]. *A modest proposal for how the bad old days will end.* [London] : Pandoras Books, Dec. 1981. 8p., ill. "The collapse of the world as we know it has already begun. Everyone knows this. Everyone feels it in their bones. All the attempts to deny it are enough to prove it." p. 1. "This article was first produced in 1975 by Reinvention of Everyday Life in California. It was reprinted in the UK by Social Revolution (who have since merged with Solidarity)." — anon, p. [8].

196.
Martin, Jim. Orgone addicts: Wilhelm Reich versus the Situationists. *Version 90.* (2), 1990, pp. 98-115, ill. ISBN 0941215075.
    An awkward look at the influence of Wilhelm Reich on the Situationists (Vaneigem in particular) and the American pro-situ groups (particularly those associated with Ken Knabb). "The crucial difference that Reich pointed out between himself and the anarchists (and this holds true for situs, libertarians, and council communists as well) was the question of the emotional capacity for freedom that the average citizen possesses ... the fundamental failure of the Situationists was their inability to confront their own characters." — Martin, pp. 114-115.

197.
Michaelson, Louis [Adam Cornford?]. *Can't buy me love: the last refuge of desire.* [S.l.]: [s.n.], [n.d.].
    One sheet, brown text on beige paper, printed both sides. "For the time, the language of eyes became the language of deeds, and the result was real community — the community of freedom." — Michaelson. Adam Cornford was a member of For Ourselves, *Reference from Bob Black correspondence.

198.
The Negative and its Use. *The negative and its use: social critique of photography, issue no. 1*. Berkeley: The Negative and Its Use, [1976]. 16 p., ill.

Contents predominantly consist of an article on the American documentary photographer Diane Arbus. Also includes a manifesto-like text 'A message from the perpetrator'. "As I produce my photography and take my life's desires seriously, I (along with my comrades) seek to catalyze a social revolution at the service of my photography, my visual poetry. I wish not the suppression but the supersession of photography by means of the social realization of its poetry and imagination."- anon., p. 15.

199.
New Morning Collective. Loaded words: a rebel's guide to Situationese. *New Morning*. (Cleveland, Ohio) February, 1973, p. 14.

*Reference from For Ourselves [173], note to thesis no. 9. "The term 'détournement', employed especially as a technical term by situationists, has been defined as the revolutionary practice 'by which the spectacle is turned back on itself, turned inside out so that it reveals its own inner workings.'" — For Ourselves.

200.
Negation. *The state and counter-revolution: what is not to be done*. Berkeley: Negation, 1972.

*Reference from For Ourselves [173], note to thesis no. 76. From the same note; "In fact, a part of the initial impetus which led to the formulation of this theory (the theory of communist egoism) arose from the personal contact of several of our founding members with the mal-practice of one of the early pro-situationist groups in Berkeley, named (appropriately) 'Contradiction', who busied themselves precisely with going around condemning, 'excluding' (excommunicating), and 'breaking with' everyone in sight in retribution for sins against various situationist anti-morals; sins such as 'being bourgeois', 'participating in spectacular life,' etc." — For Ourselves.

201.
Négation. *Lip and the self-managed counter-revolution: from Negation, no. 3.* Detroit: Black & Red, 1975. 96 p., ill.

Text translated by Peter Rachleff and Alan Wallach. "We undertook the translation of this text because we found it to be one of the most stimulating analyses of any subject we had encountered in too long a time." — Translators, p. 95. The original author is cited as Nicolas Will.

202.
Perlman, Fredy. *The reproduction of daily life.* Kalamazoo, Mich.: Black & Red; Madison, Wisconsin: Radical America, 1969. 20 p., ill.

"Capitalism is not simply the work you do for a boss who sells goods for a profit, it encompasses every aspect of everyday life, and is reproduced by our conditioned responses to it." — Perlman. Other works by Perlman include; *'Against his-story, against Leviathan'*, *'Anti-Semitism and the Beirut pogram'*, *'Anything can happen'*, *'Incoherence of the intellectual'*, *'Plunder'*, *'Revolt in Socialist Yugoslavia'*, *'The continuing appeal of Nationalism'*, *'The machine against the garden'*, and *'The strait'*. See also; Perlman, Lorraine. *Having little, being much: a chronicle of Fredy Perlman's fifty years.* Detroit: Black & Red, [n.d.]. References to these books came from *AK Distribution's 1993 catalogue*. [222]

203.
Perlman, Fredy ... [et al.]. *We called a strike and no-one came.* Detroit: Black & Red, 1973. 46 p., ill.

Reprinted from *Black & Red* (4) Christmas, 1968. A détournment of artworks from throughout history with speech bubbles telling a tale concerning Satan and a strike. "Black & Red is a subversive action. It is a new front in the world anti-capitalist struggle. It is an organic link between the theory-action of the world revolutionary movement and the action-theory of the new front." — Black & Red, inside front cover.

204.
Pointblank! Strange defeat. *No Middle Ground.*(2), Fall 1983, pp. 11-21.

Originally published by the group in October 1973. *Reference from Bob Black correspondence. They also published a magazine *Pointblank!* San Francisco, [1972-73?].

205.
Point-Blank!. Situationism. In: Juno, Andrea and Vale, V. (eds.). *Pranks!* San Francisco: Research Publications, 1987. ISBN 0940642107: pp. 176-179. (Research no. 11).

"What follows are examples of Situationist activity in the Bay Area, including a brief interview with a member of the short-lived Point-Blank! group which in 1973 plastered San Francisco with posters inquiring, 'Did you ever feel like killing your boss?', etc, bearing the Mayor's private phone number." — Research, p. 176. "... in the early '70's there were five Situationist groups in Berkeley: Point-Blank!, Diversion, Negation, Contradiction, and the Bureau of Public Secrets — all competing!" — Anon., p. 176.

206.
Sausage, Eddie Lee. Concerning psychogeography, play and the Bastille of meaning. *Snicker/Smile: magazine of multiple becomings.* (6), [1990?], pp. 14-15, ill.

A brief account of the author's interest in psychogeography. "I call for a re-evaluation of urbanity according to psychogeographic principles, the triumph of the drift as a nexus between life and art, and the repossession of 'public space' for play." — Sausage, p. 15. This *Smile* although it has a different title is from the same people producing the *Smile* below. For a brief overview of the Smile phenomenon see my *Smile classified*. [253]

207.
Shiz-flux. The totality for kids. *Smile.* (2), [1988?]. 24 p., ill.

A special edition that collects together anonymous articles adapting Situationist theory. Contents include: 'Socialism or barbarism', 'The totality for kids', and 'The society of the spectacle'. This *Smile* was produced by Shiz-flux, Smile, Box 3502, Madison WI 53704.

208.
Situationist Liberation Front. *Parlez vous Français? G.E Debord.* [S.l.]: Adhoc coalition of concerned situationist committees struggling against our oppression, [n.d.]. A4 sheet printed one side, ill.

Jokey poster aimed at satirizing the Situationist milieu. "The Situationists are an oppressed minority of intellectuals, shop-lifters, publishers, students and even workers."

209.
Shutes, Chris and Isaac Cronin. *Skirmishes with an untimely man: a critique of Diversion*. Berkeley and San Francisco: Chris Shutes and Isaac Cronin, May, 1974. 10 p.

Critique of *Diversion 1*, 1973. Horelick, Jon. 'ed'. "The central weakness of *Diversion #1* — and the one from which all the other weaknesses follow — is that its author, Jon Horelick, is everywhere behind the times, out of date." — p. 1.

210.
Shutes, Chris and Gina Rosenberg. *Disinterest compounded daily: a critique of Point-Blank as a revolutionary organization and a few proposals for the supersession of Situationism*. Berkeley: Gina Rosenberg and Chris Shutes, August 1974. 27 p., ill.

"Between the idea and the reality, between the motion and the act falls the shadow. Between the conception and the creation. Between the emotion and the response, falls the shadow. And this is the way that Point-Blank ends not with a bang but a whimper!" — Back cover. "Chris Shutes was a member of Point-Blank from its inception in 1971 up until May, 1973. Gina Rosenberg was peripherally involved with Point-Blank in 1973, also until May." — Inside front cover.

211.
Shutes, Chris. *Phenomenonology of the subjective aspect of practical-critical activity: chapter 1 Behindism*. Berkeley: Chris Shutes, Dec 1974. 9 p.

"Comprehended as a moment in the long uneven and contradictory process of the proletariat struggling to give its theory form, behindism is actually only the absence of apparent practical-critical activity. Which is one way of saying theory is on the move." — Shutes, introduction.

212.
Shutes, Chris and Cronin, Isaac, (eds.). *Implications 1*. Berkeley: The editors, December 1975, 56 p.

"Extracts of a letter of mine of October 1973 to Jean-Pierre Voyer and others have been reprinted in Issac Cronin's and Chris Shutes's recent journal, *Implications*." — Knabb [188], p. 33 in *Bureau of Public Secrets 1*.

213.
Shutes, Chris. *Two local chapters in the spectacle of decomposition*. Berkeley: Chris Shutes, May 1979. 21 p.

Also a poster, A2, with the same title. About the suicide cult 'Peoples Temple' and about the gay scene in California. "The essential error made everywhere concerning the phenomenon of the modern cult is to pretend as though it were a complete aberration, something out of this world and fundamentally in contradiction with the existing forms of society." — Shutes, from the poster.

214.
Shutes, Chris. *On the poverty of Berkeley life: and the marginal stratum of American society in general*. Berkeley: Chris Shutes, May 1983. 52 p.

Contents: 'Berkeley isn't ripe; it's rotten', '1001 ways to avoid confronting the fact that you are a worker', 'Consumption of reform and reform of consumption: it's natural, man', 'The superficial critique of bureaucracy, or, down with authority, long live the police!', 'The culture of decomposition and the aestheticization of daily life', and 'A few recent developments in the movement to suppress the global commodity economy'.

215.
Spillers of Seed, inc. *One way to happiness*. Raleigh, USA: Spillers of Seed, [n.d.]. 10 p.

Spillers of Seed, 789 2526 Hillsborough St. Raleigh N.C. 27607. Very small photocopied booklet in the style of *Spectacular Times*. "Everyone wants to be happy! On the following pages you will discover what is one true way to real happiness. The few minutes it will take you to read this booklet could be the beginning of life in non-cyclic time for you." — Inside front cover.

216.
Thompson, S. and Nick Abraham. *South Africa 1985: the organization of power in black and white*. London: B.M. Combustion, Nov. 1985, 10 p.

Reprint of text first published in Berkeley, August, 1985. Critiques of the state, the clergy, the Black Consciousness Movement, 'AZAPO' and the 'UDF'.

217.
Voyer, Jean-Pierre. *Reich: how to use.* Berkeley: Bureau of Public Secrets,
June 1973.
Fold-out card 10 panels. A poster was also produced. First published
as; *Reich: mode d'emploi.* Paris: Éditions Champ Libre, 1971. "I published
[this] in June 1973, along with a comic poster announcing it, and
reprinted extracts of one of his letters under the title 'Discretion is the
better part of value.'" — Knabb [188], p. 31. Knabb also states it was
an unauthorised translation. There was also an English translation
by I. Ducasse Ltd., distributed by B.M. Piranha, London, 1972.
*Reference from Debord [84, (1990)], p. 66.

218.
Ward, Tom. The Situationists reconsidered: part 1. *Anarchy: a journal of
desire armed.* (29), Summer 1991, pp. 22-23.
The article is reprinted from *Cultures in contention.* Seattle: Real
Comet Press, 1985. 287 p., ill. ISBN 0941104060. An early attempt to
sketch the totality of the Situationist project. Interesting because of
the author's connection with the American scene. "Their scandalous
methods, wicked humour, intriguing graphics, — backed up, we
learned, with a well-stocked theoretical arsenal — rang true in
'modern' California and zapped many of the jaded veterans of a
Movement-gone-stale like piercing light through a dense fog." —
Ward, p. 22. Contains a reference in note no. 2; Cronin, Issac. *The
American situationists.* (Bob Black in correspondence also refers to
this as a 8-1/2" x 11" pamphlet). Tom Ward is an ex-member of For
Ourselves. The second part of this text was withdrawn from
publication in (30) by Ward. Also by Ward see; The mercurial mind
of Dwight Macdonald. *Soho Arts Weekly.* 27/6/1984, which makes
links between Macdonald and later S.I. themes.

219.
Zerzan, John, ... [et al]. *Upshot.* San Francisco: Upshot, [Mid-70's].
Various single sheet posters some with illustrations: '*On the genesis
of Art: the revolt against work*', '*All Isms Are Wasms*' [1977], '*Subtly or
unsubtly, leftists go about their universal business of trying to protect the
foundations of hierarchical society*', '*All in all, it's just another brick in the
wall*' [On the S.I.], '*An Antidote to Alienation*', '*Homemaker of Year cited
in murder*', '*Destruction through 'pollution' and the building anarchy*', '

[A grinding present is glaringly, relentlessly calling all into question...]',
'Ann Landers: an endorsement for work', ' [Why work?]' [1975], *'We have
lost our reverence: Anti-politics of a dying world', 'Landlords, bosses and
leaders are old shoes: dance barefoot'.* John, Paula, Gary. [1975]. Addresses
used: Upshot, P.O. Box 40256 San Francisco, CA. (earlier) and Upshot
P.O. Box 26135 Los Angeles, CA. 90026 (later).

220.
Zerzan, John. *Elements of refusal.* Seattle: Left Bank Books, 1988. 263 p.
ISBN 0939306085.

A collection of Zerzan's essays including 'Language origin and
meaning', 'The case against art', 'Anti-work and the struggle for
control' and a select bibliography of his work. Other books by Zerzan
include; Zerzan, John and Paula. *Breakdown: data on the decomposition
of society.* Milwaukee: Lust for Life, Feb. 1976. 8 p., ill.; and *Creation
and its enemies: The revolt against work.* Rochester, New York: Mutualist
Books, 1977. 65 p. Contains 6 articles which were later to appear in
Elements of refusal.*Reference from bibliography, p. 263. See also;
Zerzan, John, and Carnes, Alice, (eds.). *Questioning technology: a
critical anthology.* London: Freedom Press, 1988. 222 p. ISBN
0900384441.

221.
Zerzan, John. Just another brick in the wall. *Anarchy: a journal of desire
armed.* (29), Summer 1991, p. 15.

Short text (a version of the poster by same name, above) which
highlights the possible contradiction of combining councilism with
free, creative play. "How is this play councilized?" — Zerzan, p. 15.
He also criticizes the American pro-situs ("sits-come-lately") for
slipping into ultra-left politics.

5. BRITISH PRO-SITUS & MILIEU

222.
AKA Books Co-Operative. *AK Distribution 1993 catalogue.* Edinburgh: AK Press, 1993. 60 p., ill.

Large catalogue containing references, with short descriptions, of many of the items listed in this bibliography. Address; 22 Lutton Place, Edinburgh, Scotland, EH8 9PE. "AK Distribution is part of AKA Books Co-Operative Ltd, a workers' co-operative wholly owned by its members. AK Press is the publishing arm of AK ... We produce separate catalogues for second-hand books, fanzines, postcards and political audio tapes."— AK, inside front cover.

223.
Angry Brigade. *The Angry Brigade 1967-1984: documents and chronology.* London: Elephant Editions, 1985. 73 p. (Anarchist Pocket-books 3).

"Life is so boring there is nothing to do except spend all our wages on the latest skirt or shirt. Brothers and Sisters, what are your real desires? Sit in the drugstore, look distant, empty, bored, drinking some tasteless coffee? Or perhaps BLOW IT UP OR BURN IT DOWN. The only thing you can do with modern slave-houses — called boutiques — IS WRECK THEM. You can't reform profit capitalism and inhumanity. Just kick it till it breaks. Revolution." — Communique 8, The Angry Brigade. First published by Bratach Dubh Anarchist Pamphlets in 1978. Contains an introduction by Jean Weir. The S.I.'s influence on the Angry Brigade is very tenuous (one mention of the 'spectacle' in a communique) but good reading anyway. For more on the Angry Brigade see; Carr, Gordon. *The Angry Brigade: the cause and the case.* London: Gollanz, 1975. 207 p., ill. ISBN 0575019921.

224.
Anon. *It's us they're shooting in Warsaw.* London: [s.n.], 6.2.82, A3 broadsheet/poster (double sided), ill.

Translated by Lucy Forsyth and Michel Prigent "from a text some friends in Paris had done." — Forsyth, correspondence. Poster about the crack down in Poland and the Solidarity movement. The text is particularly critical of the potentially reactionary position of the Solidarity leadership.

225.

Anti-copyright. Who were the situationists? *Leisure: lies, culture, subversion, cunninglinguals issue.* (4?), [1991?], p. 21.

A short, jokey, irrelevant text trying to pass the situationists off as being a product of the French Ministry of Culture. See also; Fuller, Mathew. *Flyposter frenzy: posters from the anticopyright network.* London: Working Press, 1992. ca. 100 p., ill. ISBN 187073615X. Includes many examples of détournement.

226.

Art and Language. Ralph the situationist. *Artscribe.* (66), Nov./Dec. 1987, pp. 59-62, ill.

Art and Language for this project are Michael Baldwin and Mel Ramsden. "Martin, Strijbosch, Vaneigem and Viénet wrote that 'art can only be realized in being suppressed' and that it can 'only be suppressed in being realized.' The Situationist project obeys the same unparadoxical rule." — Art and Language, p. 62. An often humorous but uninformative critique of Situationist ideas.

227.

Bishop, Robert. *Novel.* London: Architectural Association Student Forum, 1992. 80 p.

"The following text was written between 2.52 pm of Sunday 18th October and 2.52 pm of Monday 19th October 1992. The exercise was carried out as a Dérive ... Whilst this dérive does not 'move' through the city it still includes 'this letting go and its necessary contradiction'. The rules and principles of the dérive and why it is now called a novel will be apparent during the reading of it." — Bishop, preface. Bishop sat behind a typewriter with his mouth taped for twelve hours. The novel records the conversations he had with passers-by using the typewriter.

228.

Blast: fourth catalogue of Anarchist, situationist and related anti-authoritarian ideas. Bradford: Blast, 1991. [16] p.

Mail order catalogue containing over 150 titles. "The basic principle behind Blast is that useful revolutionary publications should be available to anyone, anywhere at the cheapest possible price." — Blast. The catalogue is dated 12 October 1991 and the address supplied as Blast, Box 27, c/o 31 Manor Row, Bradford, West

Yorkshire. See also; *Pierce Magazine: Introducing a revolution.* Bradford: Blast!, March 1990. 31 p., ill. See also *Blast 3*. Bradford: Blast 1989.

229.
B.M. Blob [Dave and Stuart Wise]. *Like a summer with a thousand July's .. and other seasons.* London: B.M. Blob, 1982, 57 p. ill.

A detailed account of the 1981 riots on mainland Britain. "The summer riots of '81 were the foretaste of the future for us. One day sooner or later the roof is going to blow off the UK." — Wolfie Smith, Speed, Tucker and June, (1982), p. 56. See also; B.M. Blob [Dave and Stuart Wise]. *Report on the Danish mass strike of March and April 1985.* London: B.M. Blob, n.d.

230.
B.M. Blob [Dave and Stuart Wise] and B.M. Combustion. *France goes off the rails: the movements in France, Nov. 1986 — Jan. 1987.* London: B.M. Blob and B.M. Combustion, 1987. 43 p., ill.

"This text is the responsibility of B.M. Blob and B.M. Combustion, though several other people helped with some of the translations and information. This is the first text we've produced together ... Our specific collaboration on this does not pretend to constitute any Organisation, Association, Re-groupment, Milieu or Clique." — Inside front cover. Documentation and analysis of recent worker and student actions in France.

231.
B.M. Blob [Dave and Stuart Wise]. *Once upon a time there was a place called Notting Hill Gate...: a true story with pictures by Paddington Bear.* London: B.M. Blob, 1988, 70 p., ill.

"A critical history of the Notting Hill Carnival, Notting Hill Gate as a whole, and beyond... A place where anything can happen — this riotous ramble through Notting Hill Gate illustrates its wealth of diverse radicalism." — *Blast 3* (Bradford) Mail order-catalogue [228].

232.
B.M. Blob [Dave and Stuart Wise]. *The destruction of toytown UK.* London: B.M. Blob, 1990. 20 p., ill.

"The following is a random collection of thoughts instigated by the great Poll Tax riot of March 31st, 1990. It ranges from on the spot observations by participants, to a wider theoretical reflection ... on the profound social crises in the U.K." — Inside front cover. See also; B.M. Blob [Dave and Stuart Wise]. *Yugoslavia: capitalism and class struggle 1918 — 1967: some basic ingredients of Yugoslav ideology.* London: B.M. Blob, 1991. 32 p., ill.

233.

B.M. Blob [Dave and Stuart Wise]. *Workers of the world, tonight!* London: B.M. Blob, n.d.

"International dockers struggles of the eighties. Recent examples of workers revolutionary organisation." — *Blast 3* (Bradford) Mailorder catalogue [228]. B.M. Blob also translated Pravda 3 from Portugal (1987).

234.

[Brandt, Nick] Spontaneous Combustion. *Dialectical adventures into the unknown.* London: Spontaneous Combustion, [1974]. 38 p., ill.

Spontaneous Combustion, Box LBD, 197 Kings Cross Road, London WC1. Collaged, détourned newspaper articles and photographs. On cover "Oh no!... It can't be... But it is... It's... Generalized self-management!!!!!"

235.

[Brandt, Nick] Spontaneous Combustion. *Carry on consciousness brought to you by the makers of history: some thoughts on this and that.* London: Spontaneous Combustion, [n.d.]. 15 p.

White paper cover and text on blue paper. "Some arbitrary chronological thoughts on 'Dialectical adventures into the unknown' (printed Oct. 1974)." — inside front cover.

236.

[Brandt, Nick] B.M. Combustion. *The class struggle in South Africa, 1976.* London: B.M. Combustion, n.d.

"A short pamphlet which highlights the anti-authoritarian nature of the shanty town (and beyond) riots, dispelling the myth of 'black against black' violence as blacks attacked local institutions, pointing out that they were attacking their immediate enemies. Also a section taken from 'On the poverty of Berkeley life.'" — *Blast 3* (Bradford) Mail-order catalogue [228].

237.

[Brandt, Nick] B.M. Combustion. *Re-fuse*. London: B.M. Combustion, 1978. 44 p.

Subtitled 'Further dialectical adventures into the unknown'. "This new situationist journal is an outrageous attack on all that 'Time Out' stands for i.e. concerned left-wing journalism and critical appreciation of all that's best in entertainment. It's condemnation of everything and everyone standing in the way of each individual enjoying their passions and imaginations fully in the world around them, includes, among others, the Left (caricatured as sacrificial altruists out of touch with their experience) and the Arts (belittled as mere soporific compensations for people's lack of creativity). This little slander sheet is available from... " — review in *Time Out*, 1978, reproduced in Blazwick [11], p. 85. Also by [Brandt, Nick] B.M. Combustion. *Miner conflicts-major contradictions*. London: B.M. Combustion, 1984. 32 p. Pamphlet on the miner's strike.

238.

[Brandt, Nick] B.M. Combustion. *The misery of unions: a recent example of class consciousness in struggle: Barcelona 1979*. London: B.M. Combustion, [1984?]. 4 p., 1 A4 sheet folded.

"This has been an extract from "Get Fucked!", volume 1 out in May available from B.M. Combustion." — p. 4. I have never seen or heard of *Get fucked!* getting published.

239.

[Brandt, Nick] B.M. Combustion. *Os Cangaceiros: Freedom is the crime which contains all crimes and some texts about recent movements in France.* London: B.M. Combustion, 1986. 16 p., ill.

"A short pamphlet about the prison revolts in France during May and June, 1985. Written by a group who gave practical support to those involved in the riots by both publicising their aims and demands and extending the struggle BEYOND the prisons rather than spectating via the six o'clock news." — *Blast 3* (Bradford) Mail-order catalogue [228].

240.

[Brandt, Nick] B.M. Combustion. *Rebel violence v hierarchical violence: a chronology of anti-state violence on the UK mainland July 1985 — May 1986.* London: B.M. Combustion, 1987. 34 p., ill.

An anthology of cuttings and comments on the topic of class violence, as the title suggests.

241.
[Brandt, Nick] B.M. Combustion. *Rest in peace.* London: B.M. Combustion, n.d. "An attack on the peace movement, including a critique of CND, Greenham Common and some aspects of anarchist opposition within the movement." *Blast 3* (Bradford) Mail-order catalogue [228]. Other B.M. Combustion publications unseen include: *Alternative socialism — the manifesto of radical diplomats.* 1977. 12 p.; and *The Emin — being a critique of cultism with specific reference to 'The Emin', a patriarchal mystical group based in London.* 1977. 12 p.

242.
British Internationalists [Lucy Forsyth, Michel Prigent, Dave Wise and Stuart Wise]. *To libertarians.* London: British Internationalists, August 1981. A1 broadsheet double-sided, ill.

The text on one side 'To esteemed comrades ... ', was published anonymously in Spanish but was originally by Debord. On the imprisonment of libertarians in Spain, mostly in Segovia prison. "The struggle to set them free can be a point of departure for a new revolutionary movement, more effective and more coherent. Silence and inaction will only load shame upon us, and history will never forgive us." — Debord.

243.
Burns, Alan. *The Angry Brigade: a documentary novel.* London: Quartet, 1973. 185 p. ISBN 0704310910.

A more evocative than informative book. "This book brings together the experiences of members of two activist communes. It tells how as individuals they became radicalized, how as groups they were organised, how they related to the world outside, how they dealt with the police, how they undertook illegal and dangerous actions." — Burns, p. 2.

244.
Caribbean Situationist. *None shall escape: Caribbean Situationist against Trevor Monroe.* London: Caribbean Situationist, July, 1973. A2 size sheet, printed one side, ill.

Caribbean Situationist, B.M. Box Soon, London WCIV 6XX, England.

Includes a translation of thesis no. 90 from *Society of the spectacle* [91] and an excerpt from Vaneigem's *Revolution of everyday life*. [142]

245.
Caribbean Situationist [Fundi]. *None shall escape: radical perspectives in the Caribbean*. London: News From Everywhere, 1988. 21 p., ill.

First published in *No Middle Ground*, San Francisco. 1984. Contents: 'Radical perspectives in the Caribbean', 'What Padmore passed through,' and 'The adventure of Westmoreland'. "The following is a compilation of excerpts from a forum on Grenada and Jamaica, which was held in San Francisco in December, 1983, follow-up interviews and informal discussions. The edited statements belong to a 53-year-old Jamaican named Fundi." — Anon, p. 3. This edition also included a colour map of the Caribbean detailing scenes of revolt. The address for News From Everywhere is given as; Box 14, 136 Kingsland High Street, London E 8.

246.
Christiana (ed.). *Cabaret: an anthology of political buffoonery 1980-88*. Leeds: [Agit Press?], [1989?]. [48] p., ill.

"The stories which follow are all 'acts' of political cabaret played in the theatre of life. Acts of political buffoonery be it planned or accidental recorded for posterity in the hope that they might inspire." Christiana, introduction, p. 1.

247.
Chronos Publications Catalogue 1986. [Lucy Forsyth, Michel Prigent, et al.?] 1 A4 sheet folded.

Includes reference to the following texts not listed elsewhere in this bibliography. "*On the New Cross fire by a friend of Junius* written in March 1981. It deals with the horrific fire in which 13 young died. *Ripple Press*. 50 p[ence]. ... *The Class Struggles in Airstrip One by a friend of Junius*, written during the Miners' strike of 1984. *Ripple Press*. 70 p[ence]. *A critique of 'Call it Sleep' to wake you up*. 1985. 30 p[ence]. (About the video by Cronin & Seltzer). ...*Mercurius Fumigosus or the Smoking Nocturnal communicating dark and hidden newes* [sic] by a friend of Junius, May 1st 1985. *Ripple Press*. On the same day *The Thunderer no 1* was also distributed by a friend. 40 p[ence] each." — from the catalogue *[as in original text]*. Michel Prigent acting under various names and through various publications has been a consistently antagonistic and often hilarious commentator on things Situationist, particularly the ICA show and Tate Gallery events. Prigent and Lucy Forsyth (publishing under the Chronos imprint) have also carried out much important work on the translation of key texts by Debord.

248.
Cornuault, Joël. *Confidential report on practical hope (from the graveyard of the present to the construction of situations really worth living)*. London: B.M. Combustion, [1978]. 7 p.

Translation of; Cornuault, Joël. Pour le passage de la decomposition a des constructions nouvelles. *Les raisons de la colere*. (1), Paris, 1978. Another work involving Cornuault, Bloch, and Peres is *Revolutionary theory for beginners*, *Reference supplied by the Museum of Modern Prehistory, correspondence.

249.
Cosgrove, Stuart. Spectacle: a guide through the menu of Situationism. *I D Magazine*. (58), May 1988, pp. 52-56, ill.

'Story by Stuart Cosgrove.' And story it is. A confusionist mish-mash based on half-truths and inaccuracies. Trying to link the S.I. to everything from the Animal Liberation Front to the "situationist comedy [of] Jerry 'Gobshite' Sadowitz." "Situationism is a movement, an attitude and a radical pose. It thrives on political mischief, on pranksterism, on the corruption and inversion of society's own rituals, customs, ceremonies and 'spectacles', in order to make a political statement *against* society." — Cosgrove, p. 52. The article was produced for the *I D Magazine* 'Revolution issue.'

250.
Desire in ruins: an installation of works by Glyn Banks/Hannah Vowles, Ed Baxter, Simon Dickason, Karen Eliot, Andy Hopton, Stefan Szczelkun. Glasgow: Transmission Gallery, 1987. Single sheet folded to make 16 pages.

Catalogue of the exhibition held at the Transmission Gallery May 5th-May 30th, 1987. Texts by Bob Jones, Karen Eliot [Stewart Home], Stefan Szczelkun, Ed Baxter and 'Strategic textual appropriations from the *Postmodern scene* (Kroker and Cook), *The Guardian*, Barbara Cartland and the first lady of country music, Tammy Wynette' by Art in Ruins.

251.

Downham, Mark. Videodrome: the thing in room 101. *Vague*. (17/18), [1987], pp. 6-11.

Also published in; Dwyer, Simon, (ed.). *Rapid Eye: art, occult, cinema, music.* Brighton: Rapid Eye, 1989. ISBN 09513161805: pp. 185-191. "Situationism. A political dada that identified and described the Society of the 'Spectacle' and invented a perception to deal with it. Over two decades after the Student riots that it provoked, Mark Downham argues that the Spectacle has absorbed the Situationist's original revolutionary perception and re-sequenced itself to absorb and 'recuperate' any such threats. The Spectacle is Control, the experience of a false perception of reality. We are children of the Videodrome, and nobody owns Death TV." — Introduction in *Rapid Eye*, p. 185. A dérive through assorted Situationist and pro-situ quotations. "The videodrome is the update, the charnel house of spectacular subliminal language." — Downham.

252.

Exeter and Earth Theatre of Postmodernism. *Manifesto of the revived Situationist International.* Exeter: [s.n.], [1989]. 1 p.

Word processed text/flyer. Here is part of the text for all it is worth. "1) Marx. 2) Derri-dada. 3) Debord. 4) Blake. 5) Workers' councils. 6) Better spectacles. 7) Situational internationalism and international situations. Methods: Drift — if we do not know where we are going, they will never be able to track us down. Turning — WE will take THEIR artefacts and turn them to our use. Situations — transformations of people into art as they live, not after they've lived. 'We, the revived etc. declare that we are libidinal intensities and organless bodies flowing freely through the streets of Exeter and the Earth. We flow for the good of the planet and anyone who impedes our progress we denounce as reactionary, opportunist. We reject the rigours of Lenin-Trotsykism: we will not see our spectacles circumscribed by frames ... If anyone says we exist, she is lying.'"

253.

Ford, Simon. *Smile classified.* London: National Art Library, Victoria and Albert Museum, 1992. 10 p.

A pamphlet produced to accompany an exhibition at the National Art Library, Victoria and Albert Museum from 20 March to 10

August 1992. It comprises of a brief overview of the confusing terrain of the *Smile* phenomenon including an extensive bibliography by Monty Cantsin ('Smile history lesson'). For another, slightly inaccurate account of *Smile* see; Kester, Grant. Art Press review: Smile. *New Art Examiner*, Oct. 1987. pp. 17-18.

254.
Fountain, Nigel. *Underground: the London alternative press, 1966-74.* London: Routledge, 1988. 251 p., ill. ISBN 0415007283.

"That spring the slow march of the Situationists through the London of the decade surfaced on the cover of *It* [International Times] 26, with a situationist poster ... Dave Robins had been in touch with the group, and was to share a house with one of their then leading London lights, Chris Grey [sic] ... It was an appealing image, and an appealing movement for radicals hunting their red snark, and tired of waiting for Godot. It promised involvement, rationalized non-organization, it dramatized outcast status, and offered the possibility of action, and, as the next decade opened, provided it for a few. It also endorsed the hostility which many of those radicals felt for the orthodox left. It would be propaganda of the deed, if, for many, it remained words. It also provided another link between the radicals and the radicalized hippies." —Fountain, pp. 58-59. For another look at the British underground press see; Nelson, Elizabeth. *The British counter-culture, 1966-73: a study of the underground press.* Basingstoke: Macmillan, 1989. 182 p. ISBN 0333429230; and Spiers, John, (ed.). *The underground and alternative press in Britain: bibliographical guide with historical notes.* Brighton: Harvester, 1974. 77 p. ISBN 0901759848. For information about the American underground press see; Lewis, Roger. *Outlaws of America: the underground press and its context.* Harmondsworth: Penguin, 1972. 204, [4] p., ill. ISBN 0140215867 ; Peck, Abe. *Uncovering the sixties: the life and times of the underground press.* New York: Citadel Press, 1991 (1985). xviii, 378 p., ill. ISBN 0806512253; and Leamer, Laurence. *The paper revolutionaries: the rise of the underground press.* New York: Simon & Schuster, [1972]. 220 p., ill. ISBN 0671211439.

255.

Frith, Simon and Horne, Howard. *Art into pop*. London: Methuen, 1987. 206 p., ill. ISBN 041641530X hbk. and 0416415407 pbk.

A study of the influence of art schools and art students on post-war British popular music. "McLaren's importance was to make pop situationism the most convincing *explanation* of the maelstrom in which the Sex Pistols found themselves — convincing not to mainstream cultural commentators (for whom 'dole queue rock' was a sufficient label) but to punk musicians themselves and to their hippest observers." — Frith, pp. 132-133. See especially chapter 4, 'The pop situationists' — pp. 123-161.

256.

Green Jonathan. *Days in the life: voices from the English Underground 1961-1971*. London: Minerva, 1989. 468 p. ISBN 0749390123.

First hand accounts of life in the sixties. Contains a few references to the S.I., the Angry Brigade and King Mob. "When we met the Situationists, in '67, we realised this was what we wanted. When the LSE [London School of Economics] occupation happened it was a total free-for-all ... And we were so impressed by this guy that after they'd thrown him out we sought him out on the steps of the main LSE building, and it was John Gravelle. He was just meeting Chris Gray and Don Nicholson-Smith who were the British wing of the Situationists ... So all these people, based in Notting Hill came together and gradually formed this group called King Mob which was expelled from [the] Situationist International for being a sect. They wouldn't tolerate any kind of tendencies or whatever and also our take was different from theirs: they were high-powered French intellectuals, we were rapidly becoming street hippies." — Dick Pountain, pp. 249-250.

257.

[Hanson, Tod]. *Blah, Blah: blatant lunacy and hope*. [S.l.: s.n., 1987?] [8] p., ill.

A compilation of work from *Spectacular Times*, The Last International [Bob Black], Debord, etc. "Acting the fool is a political act. When pomposity and over-seriousness reigns it is left to the fool to be the voice of sanity." p. [8].

258.
Here and Now: a magazine of radical ideas. 1- , 1985 — .

A magazine with production that alternates between the Leeds and Scottish collectives. It has regularly featured Situationist themes but is generally critical of their theory and practice. Addresses: *Here and Now*, c/o Transmission Gallery, 28 King St., Glasgow G1 5QP or *Here and Now*, P.O. Box 109, Leeds, LS5 3AA. In particular see; McIntyre, Calum. The arena of discontent. *Here and Now.* (1), Spring 1985, pp. 7-9; The Pleasure Tendency. The subversive past. *Here and Now.* (2), Summer 1985, pp. 10-11; Home, Stewart. Fetishisation. *Here and Now.* (6), 1987. p. 19. [Unauthorized publication of correspondence.]; Branchflower, George. Oranges and Lemons. *Here and Now.* (7/8), 1989, pp. vii-ix; Art/Anti-Art Supplement. *Here and Now.* (10), 1990, pp. i-xvi; Mr. Jones. Artistic disarmament (Art Strike). *Here and Now.* (11), pp. 23-25; Stephen Small and Steve Bushell. Letters. *Here and Now* . (13), 1992, pp. 29.

259.
Hewison, Robert. *Too much: art and society in the sixties: 1960-75.* London: Methuen, 1986. xviii, 350 p., ill. ISBN 0413608808.

Describes the counter-cultural scene (particularly the underground press) in Britain during the sixties and early seventies. Brief mentions of the S.I.'s 'influence' on Trocchi and the May '68 events.

260.
Home, Stewart, (ed.). *Plagiarism: art as commodity and strategies for its negation.* London: Aporia Press, 1987. [44] p. ISBN 0948518871.

"This is a pamphlet intended to accompany the debate that surrounds 'The Festival of Plagiarism', but it may also be read and used separately from any specific event." — Home, p. 1. A collection of texts on and around the idea of plagiarism. Includes; 'Plagiarism' by Ralph Rumney; 'Plagiarism, culture, mass media' by Klaos Oldanburg [Stewart Home]; and 'Re.Distribution' by Waldemar Jyroczech [Ed Baxter]. A review of the festival also appeared as; Baxter, Ed. A footnote to the Festival of Plagiarism. *Variant.* (5), Summer/Autumn 1988, pp. 26-28.

261.

Home, Stewart. Aesthetics and resistance, totality reconsidered. *Smile.* (11), 1989, p. 2.

Notes made for a panel discussion at the I.C.A. 24/6/89. "I would suggest that there is no question of specto-Situationist ideas having been recuperated by a 'spectacular' (or indeed any other sort of) society. To suggest that situationist theory has been hijacked by the capitalist media is to credit the former with a critical rigour it did not achieve and the latter with a totalising power it does not possess." — p. [2].

262.

Home, Stewart. *The Festival of Plagiarism.* London: Sabotage Editions, 1989, 24 p., [16] p. of ill. ISBN 0951441701.

"In as much as this is a 'critical' piece of writing, it is concerned with some of the ways in which various individuals responded to the issues raised by the Festival of Plagiarism. While I offer a description of the entire Festival, this description should not be taken as constituting any in-depth 'aesthetic judgement'. Pure aesthetics, were such a thing possible, would not in any case interest me. The description I offer is intended largely for informational purposes (to provide a 'record' of what took place)." — Home, p. 1.

263.

Home, Stewart, (ed.). *Art Strike handbook.* London: Sabotage Editions, 1989. 40 p. ISBN 095144171X.

"We call on all cultural workers to put down their tools and cease to make, distribute, sell, exhibit, or discuss their work from January 1st 1990 to January 1st 1993. We call for all galleries, museums, agencies, 'alternative' spaces, periodicals, theatres, art schools, etc., to cease all operations for the same period." — Home, p. 1. An anthology of texts, some directly concerning the controversial Art Strike 1990-1993, and others included "to place the strike in a broader context" (which includes critiques of the Situationist stance on art).

264.

Home, Stewart. *Pure mania.* Edinburgh: Polygon, 1989. 217 p. ISBN 0748660356. (Polygon Sigma; 2.)

"*Pure mania* is set in an almost fictional anarcho-punk milieu around the council estates of London's East End. In part a trashy adventure story and in part a blatantly falsified tour of eighties youth trends and subcultural politics..." — Inside front cover.

265.

Home, Stewart. Marx, Christ and Satan united in struggle: Stewart Home interviewed by Karen Goaman. *Variant*. (7), 1989, pp. 19-23, ill.

A revealing interview with Stewart Home, a critical but major figure in the revival of interest in things Situationist. "I wanted the book [31] to be a kind of bluff-your-way guide, to deprive these ex-public school boys within the anarchist movement of their specialist knowledge ... when I looked into the group [the Situationists] I found that most of their ideas could be traced back to other sources such as Dada, Cobra, Marx, the Frankfurt School, Henri Lefebvre, Lukàcs and so on." — Home, p. 20. For another interview with Stewart Home see; Where have all the boot boys gone. *Fist*. (3), 1990, p. 6.

266.

Home, Stewart. *Defiant pose*. London: Peter Owen, 1991. 167 p. ISBN 0720608287.

A fictional account of skinhead Terry Blake's revolutionary adventures in contemporary London. A détournement of Richard Allen's popular New English Library series of cult youth pulp such as *Skinhead* and *Suedehead*. Includes the hilariously inept pro-situ group 'My One Flesh', perhaps the first appearance of Situationist theory in an English language novel?

267.

Home, Stewart. *Neoist manifestos*. Stirling: AK Press, 1991, [128] p. ISBN 1873176155

Tête-bêche. Reprints of texts from *Smile* 1-8, 1984-87. Includes a short autobiography 'To tell the truth' (updated and reprinted from *Lightworks*. (?) 1987, pp. 30-32, ill.), 16 manifestos and an appendix of Home's poetry. Turn the book over and it becomes; Mannox, James, (ed.). *Art strike papers*. "The Art strike papers is a substantial collection of material produced in response to the Art Strike 1990-93. It is made up entirely of pieces which have appeared since the publication of the *Art strike handbook* in April 1989." — Introduction. Stewart Home's *Smile* magazine went on to issue 11 when it was suspended due to Art Strike 1990-93. For information on another art strike see;

Dordevic, Goran. *The international strike of artists?* [Berlin]: [Museum für (Sub-) Kultur, Fuldastrasse 33, 1000 Berlin 44], 1979. 50 p., ill. For more (mis)information on Neoism see also; Scott, Pete. What's there to smile about: the Neoist cultural conspiracy. *Vague*. no. 18-19, pp. 117-123; Scott, Pete. Neoism. In: Dwyer [252], pp. 48-51; and Cantsin, Monty, [Haufen, Graf,] (ed.). *Neoism now: the first Neoist anthology and sourcebook*. Berlin: Artcore Editions, [1987]. [ca. 140] p., ill. Artcore Editions, Weisestr. 58, 1000 Berlin 44, Germany.

268.

Law, Larry. *A true historie & account of the pyrate Captain Misson, his crew & their colony of Libertatia founded on peoples rights & liberty on the island of Madagascar: the story of Misson and Libertatia.* [London]: Spectacular Times, 1980 (reprinted in 1991). 29 p., ill.

A reprint arranged by A Distribution and Dark Star Press. "[The publication] is an account of an early attempt by a group of people to build a genuinely libertarian and egalitarian community. A community which attempted to live by the maxim 'Liberty, Equality, Fraternity' nearly one hundred years before the French Revolution." — Law, p. 5.

269.

Law, Larry, (ed.). *Buffo: amazing tales of political pranks and anarchic buffoonery; no. (1/2).* London: Spectacular Times, 1985 (reprinted 1988). 36 p., ill. ISBN 0907837093.

Includes sections on détournement ("Subversion — the devaluation and re-use of present and past cultural production, destroying its message while hijacking its impact." — Law, p. 2.), elections, stamps and banknotes, the media, art, and shopping. First published as; *Buffo!: a short anthology of political pranks and anarchic buffoonery.* London: Spectacular Times, [1982]. [26] p., ill. ISBN 0907837026.

270.

Law, Larry and Dunbar, Linny and Dunnington, Jo. *Are you in a bad state?* London: Spectacular Times, [n.d.]. Video, 40 mins.

In *Bigger cages, longer chains* [281] this is described as "A helter-skelter ride from the dawn of pre-history to the present day. Funny and serious by turns. TV will never seem the same again." Highlight is a collection of news clips, graphically illustrating police brutality, combined with the song 'The laughing policeman'.

271.

Law, Larry. *Images*. London: Spectacular Times, 1979. 16 p., ill. (Pocketbook series no. 1.)

The first in the series looks at the Spectacle using the now familiar technique of handwritten text combined with quotations and cuttings. "We live in a Spectacular Society. That is, our whole life is surrounded by an immense accumulation of Spectacles. Things that were once lived directly are now lived by proxy." — p. [2]. Law's *Spectacular Times* pocketbook series have been influential in the popularisation and the Anglicisation of S.I. ideas.

272.

Law, Larry. *Everyday life*. London: Spectacular Times, 1979. 16 p., ill. (Pocketbook series no. 2.)

"We start to dismantle the Spectacle by seizing back from the authorities the power to run our own lives. Once again to take control of the organisation of everyday life ourselves — be it at individual level, in our home, our street, at our place of work or in our community." — p. [13]. *Everyday life* and *Images* have been reprinted in one volume by A Distribution in 1993.

273.

Law, Larry (and production by Liz). *The media*. London: Spectacular Times, 1980. 24 p., ill. (Pocketbook series no. 3.)

"The Spectacle is not just a collection of images. It is the medium of communication between images and is the means by which the real world is interpreted. The mass media is Spectacular. Even in extremis it is unable to see itself as a participant in real life. Instead it turns real life into a Spectacle — and participates in that." — pp. 2-5. Reprinted by A Distribution in 1993.

274.

Law. Larry. *Fin de spectacle*. London: Spectacular Times, 1980. 22 p., ill. (Pocketbook series no. 4.)

"It is hard not to notice that something is going on. The Spectacle is turning in on itself — it watches for every minute sign of its own deterioration. Having no future — it turns in on its past. It attempts to beautify itself — but only succeeds in making itself even more grotesque." — Law.

275.
[Law, Larry, trans.] Ehrlich, Carol. *Women and the spectacle*. London: Spectacular Times, 1981. 16 p., ill. (Pocketbook series no. 7.)

"This article ... is part of a longer work entitled *Socialism, Anarchism & Feminism*, which was first published by Research Group One (USA) in 1977. ... This edition published in 1992 by A Distribution." — p. [2].

276.
Law, Larry. *The spectacle: a skeleton key*. London: Spectacular Times, n.d. 24 p., ill. ISBN 0907837018. (Pocketbook series no. 8[/9].)

On the Spectacle and Urbanism. "The Spectacle fills not only time but space as well. It is our environment. The control of our environment has been taken from us and put into the hands of specialists ... their object is to organise the environment into more manageable structures." — Law, p. 18.

277.
Law, Larry. *Animals*. Revised edition. London: Spectacular Times, 1986. [48] p., ill. ISBN 0907837042. (Pocketbook series no. 10.)

First edition published in 1982. "If enslavement begins with humans it must end with the simultaneous liberation of humans and animals from the yoke of commodity fetishism and narcissistic effusions." — Law. A collage of cuttings and quotes on the theme of animal liberation.

278.
Law, Larry. *More of the shame*. London: Spectacular Times, 1983. [32] p., ill. (Pocketbook series no. 11.)

Overview of the state of the spectacle in the usual format of cuttings from newspapers and quotes from S.I. and pro-situ texts.

279.
Law, Larry. *The bad days will end*. London: Spectacular Times, 1983. 30 p., ill. [ISBN 0907837077 for reprint published by A Distribution, 1992]. (Pocketbook series no. 12)

"From the starting point 'the real state secret is the secret misery of daily life', this pocketbook dumps ideology on its way to revolutionary theory firmly based on the pleasure principle. The text constantly returns to the theme of dreams, desires, hopes, feelings, love, pleasure and playfulness — words which disappeared long ago from the vocabulary of 'serious' political writers." — Spectacular Times publicity material in *Vague* (18/19). In the *Negative and its Use* [198], (p. 14) this is credited to Charles Lutwidge, "A six-page newspaper dealing with how we can get out of this nightmare and start playing," and dated 1975.

280.
Law, Larry. *Cities of illusion*. London: Spectacular Times, 1984. [48] p., ill. (Pocketbook series no. 13.) ISBN 0907837085.
Press cuttings and quotes taken from many diverse sources on the theme of ideology. "In the Society of the Spectacle we live in a world of carefully constructed illusions — about ourselves, each other, about power, authority, justice and daily life." — Law.

281.
Law, Larry. *Bigger cages, longer chains*. London: Spectacular Times, 1987. [70] p., ill. ISBN 0907837123. (Pocketbook series no. 14.)
"The world is full of ideologies that claim to offer freedom, but in reality simply offer us bigger cages and longer chains. The demand for an end to cages and chains may seem idealistic to some people, but the real idealists are those who think we can carry on as we are." — Law. Quotations interspersed with Law's handwritten text on the theme of freedom. Other Pocketbooks may have included the following; *Food* and *Into the endgame*.

282.
Le Brun, Annie. *Vagit-Prop*. London: B.M. Chronos, 1986. 5 p.
Translated by Lucy Forsyth and Michel Prigent on June 30, 1986. "Colour Supplement to *The Horse's Mouth No. 1*". This text first appeared in *Le Monde* Dec. 6 1984. The text is subtitled "The television adaption of the 'Second sex', by Simone de Beauvoir, and Marguerite Duras's works considered as monuments of a state feminism..." See also; Le Brun, Annie. *Vagit-prop: lâcheté tout: et autres textes*. Paris: Ramsay/J.-J. Pauvert, 1990. 273 p. ISBN 2859568611.

283.

London Psychogeographical Association and the Archaeogeodetic Association. *The great conjunction: the symbols of a college the death of a king and the maze on the hill.* London: Unpopular Books, 1992. 31 p., ill. ISBN 1871593050.

"The London Psychogeographical Association was founded in July 1957 in Cosio d'Arroscia. It swiftly fused with the Situationniste Internationale. It was revived August 1992 as a completely independent organisation. This was celebrated with a cycle trip to the cave at Roisia's Cross, at Royston, to coincide with the conjunction of Venus and Jupiter." — Backcover. The L.P.A.'s latest publication is: Jorn, Asger. *Open creation and its enemeies* ... Calanais, Alba: L.P.A., 1993. 31 p., ill. ISBN 1871593107.

284.

Murray, John. *From art for a living to living art.* [London: Open Eye], 1989. [16] p.

This text was available from the short lived *Open Eye* magazine upon request. "Unrevised reprint of draft article by John Murray ... the S.I. was at this time getting 'trendy'... this article is intended as an explanation of the S.I. in as journalistic a style as possible." — Editorial. "The only way in which they could have put the best aspects of their theory into practice would have been to devolve into autonomous individuals. The S.I. had become a constraint on autonomy, with its strict codes of discipline and conduct and its existence as an organisation." — Murray.

285.

Neon Lights: number 1. Manchester: Grass Roots Bookshop (printed by Moss Side Press Ltd.), [n.d.]. 23 p., ill.

A4 format magazine. Contents include Vaneigem on roles, Ten days that shook the university, bureaucratic comics, and a conversation with Stalin. Ten days that shook the university was typed by Sue Clark and Chris Trench translated it.

286.

Nominal Agency. Suckers for pretension. *The Agent.* (5), Spring, 1987, pp. 22-23.

Jokey discussion between an estate agent and a Zen Situationist.

287.

Pleasure Tendency. *Life and its replacement with a dull reflection of itself: preliminary theses of the Pleasure Tendency*. Leeds: The Pleasure Tendency, June 1984. 40 p.

> Small booklet with small type. "The Pleasure Tendency is ... Civilisation dreaming ... We must look forward to the time when merely taking a walk outside tickles the pleasure centre. When the deluge of falsified experience recedes, when the few books which are still read are those which stimulate debate, enhance learning and inspire action. When all life is lived intensely, or passes exactly, as one would wish. When the parasite Art is no more." — Pleasure Tendency.

288.

Pleasure Tendency. *Desire-Value and the Pleasure Tendency: two essays from the Pleasure Tendency: further theses: 1*. Leeds: Pleasure Tendency, Oct. 1985. 22 p. ISBN 0948688017.

> "Pleasure Tendency (1) The expression of the pleasure principle whereby the fulfilment of desire is pursued in a direct and unmediated manner and in a manner which recognises the social interdependence between such a principle and the pleasure of other individuals. (2) The name of the group seeking to propagate these ideas in their social, political and temporal context." — Pleasure Tendency.

289.

Pleasure Tendency. *The subversive past: two essays from the Pleasure Tendency: further theses: 2*. Leeds: Pleasure Tendency, Oct. 1985. 19 p. ISBN 0948688025.

> Although no mention is made of any S.I. influence, these pamphlets are close to the S.I. tradition because of their dense critiques of consumer society. In the main essay 'Decline of pleasure; rise of leisure' pleasure is defined as "self-determination and un-paid for enjoyment" whilst leisure is "managed, mediated and paid-for recreation."

290.

Pleasure Tendency. *Return of the moral subject: an essay on class identity and free will from the Pleasure Tendency: further theses: 3*. Leeds: Pleasure Tendency, Sept. 1986. 26p., ill. ISBN 0948688033.

Contains three chapters; 'Introduction', 'The philosophical basis', 'Class and struggle' and an appendix, 'The place of dialectics in the understanding'. The booklet ends with the thought that "the power of the imagination is the equal of whatever reality it encounters."

291.
Pleasure Tendency. *Theses against cynicism*. Leeds: Pleasure Tendency, May 1987. 34p., ill. ISBN 0948688041.

"Cynicism deserves to be made an object of its own ruthless scrutiny, to make it disclose what it is meant to suppress. In the light of criticism, cynicism stands revealed as the disease of which it claims to be the diagnosis." — Pleasure Tendency.

292.
Poyner, Rick. *Nigel Coates: the city in motion*. London: Fourth Estate, 1989. 112 p., ill. ISBN 094779574X. (Blueprint monograph).

An introductory book on the British architect influenced by Situationist theory and designer of the Situationist exhibition at the I.C.A. Also by Coates see; *NATO* (1983-85). Albion issue (1983), Apprentice issue (1984), and Gamma City issue (1985). *Reference from Sussman [57], p. 194. See also; Coates, Nigel. Street signs. In : Thackara, J. (ed.). *Design after modernism*. London: Thames and Hudson, 1988, pp. 95-114; *Nigel Coates: ArkAlbion and six other projects*. London: Architectural Association [A.A.], 1984. 48 p., ill. ISBN 0904503550. Published to co-incide with an exhibition at the A.A. from October 3rd to 27th 1984; and *Ecstacity*. London: A.A., 1992. [55] p., ill. ISBN 1870890221. Exhibition held at the A.A. between May 14th to June 26th 1992. Issued in a two-piece white paper box.

293.
[Prigent, Michel] A Friend of Junius. *Biography of the anthologer considered in his past present and future*. London: B.M. Chronos, 1982. 8 p. One sheet folded.

A classic piece of Prigent invective occasioned by the publication of Knabb's *Situationist International anthology* [35]. The main criticisms are against his editorial policy, his translation and his criticism of the later S.I. texts. There is also comment on Knabb's views of religion and his involvement with the publication of *Theory of misery/misery of theory* [169].

294.

[Prigent, Michel]. *The Thunderer: issue no. 1.* Box 7, The Other Branch, 12 Gloucester Street, Leamington Spa, Warks.: [Prigent], 1985. 4 p., ill.

One A3 Sheet folded. "If [Larry] Law really wants to make a 'Situationists for beginners' why doesn't he contact the marxist-leninists at Writers and Readers ... This is a taster of a new journal ... written somewhere in the 'U.K.' 3rd May 1985."- [Prigent]. "*The Thunderer* was the original name of what has now become *The Murdock.* ... But now newspapers and magazines, in Britain, worth reading are very few; we will name one: *The Sprint.*" — [italics in original], back cover.

295.

[Prigent, Michel]. *A critical review of decomposition in Britain in 1986.* London: B.M. Chronos, 1986, 7 p., ill.

Polemic around Jamie Reid's March 1986 show at Hamiltons Gallery, London. Reid also had an exhibition at the Brixton Gallery in Atlantic Road in 1983.

296.

[Prigent, Michel]. *A brief introduction to the critique of art history and other subjects: twenty years after publication.* London: B.M. Chronos, 1988. 6 p., ill.

Produced to coincide with the Tate Gallery's series of talks and films (entitled 'Total dissent: art, culture and politics around 1968' 1-19 June 1988), especially a lecture by David Dunbar, 'The parallel avant-gardes: the Situationist International versus Situationism in the late 60s' — 14 June 1988. "For us it is a matter of defending the S.I. against embalmers like him, but above all it is a question of understanding the necessity of advancing proletarian theory and practice. A task beyond all the art historians who can only pick over the bones left by others." — Prigent, p. 3. For an alternative reading of the event see Dick Arlen [Stewart Home]. Total dissent. *Vague.* (20), 1988, p. 96.

297.

[Prigent, Michel]. *The misadventures of the Situationist International in the Temple of Doom.* London: The Reception Committee c/o B.M. Chronos, 22/6/1989. 2 p., ill.

Leaflet distributed outside the I.C.A. London during the Situationist exhibition. "For many years the S.I. itself was the subject of a cover-up by all and sundry as no one dare speak of its existence. Nowadays so many are queueing-up to offer their unwanted thoughts on the subject, that it is in danger of being buried under an avalanche of crap." — Prigent, p. 2.

298.
[Prigent, Michel]. *K-Y no.1: Special Xmas number*. London: B.M. Chronos, 1991. [5] p.

"Everything you wanted to know about the pomo-structuro-semiologo-Leninist swamp but were afraid to ask your lecturer cop." Rant against 'left wing' publishers and academics. Prigent has also been a member of the pro-situ groups 'Isadore Ducasse'/'Ducasses', 'Piranha' (1972—1976) and 'Big Brothers Anonymous' [Prigent and Mike Bradley] who produced *Catalyst Times*. *Reference from George Robertson [303]. One Piranha text was; London Situationism. *An Open letter to the S.P.G.B.* London: Piranha, [n.d.]. *Reference Barry Pateman correspondence.

299.
Reid, Jamie, ... [et al]. *Surburban Press poster book*. 1974.

"This book, which collected graphics done over the previous two years, contains fifteen posters: it was hoped that the immediacy of the poster format would increase each image's effectiveness." *Reference, from Reid [301], p. 38.

300.
Reid, Jamie, ... [et al] (eds.). *Surburban Press*. (Croydon) 1-6, 1970-1975.

"Journal on surburbia and consumer life published by Jeremy Brook, Jamie Reid, and Nigel Edwards." — Marcus [42], p. 460. "From rather naive beginnings it very quickly settled into the shit-stirring format, with thorough research into local politics and council corruption, mixed with my graphics and some Situationist texts." — Reid [301], p. 35. Circulation eventually reached 5000 copies.

301.
Reid, Jamie, and Savage, Jon. *Up they rise: the incomplete works of Jamie Reid*. London: Faber and Faber, 1987. 144p., ill. ISBN 0571147623.

A retrospective look at Reid's life and work from the 1950s to *Leaving the Twentieth Century* [26] via *Surburban Press* and the Sex Pistols graphics. Traces the roots of many of the images Reid is famous for. "Even though it's hung around my neck ever since, I was never involved with the Situationists to the fullest extent because I couldn't understand half of what they had written. I found Situationist texts to be full of jargon — almost victims of what they were trying to attack — and you had to be really well-educated to be able to understand them. I was trying to put over the waffle in a visual form; trying, say, to summarize a whole chapter of a book in one image." — Reid, p. 38.

302.
Reid, Jamie. Style sucks. *Vague*. (21), 1988, pp. 66-67.
Manifesto-like text arguing that "Never has there been such a profusion of visual communication in the media, and never has its content been more superficial and establishment/consumer orientated ... The role of the arts is to liberate the spirit and the imagination; to create a new counter culture." — Reid, pp. 66-67.

303.
Robertson, George. The Situationist International: its penetration into British Culture. *Block*. (14), Autumn 1988, pp. 39-53, ill.
Excellent and full account of the S.I. influence on the UK scene. Also covers European groups such as Provo and Kommune 1, and in the USA, Black Mask and the Motherfuckers. "I want to examine the conditions and currents from which it [the UK scene] evolved, to locate them historically, socially and culturally, and to identify the concepts and frameworks within which the Situationist project was formulated." —Robertson. A magazine not mentioned by Robertson was *The Sprint* produced in the early 80s by Nick Holliman. *Lucy Forsyth, correspondence.

304.
Ruins of Glamour/Glamour of Ruins. London: Unpopular Books, 1986. [56] p., ill.
A booklet produced to accompany the 'Ruins of Glamour/Glamour of Ruins' exhibition held at the Chisenhale Studios, December 3-20, 1986. Participants were Glyn Banks/Hannah Vowles [Art in Ruins], Ed Baxter, Simon Dickason, Karen Eliot [Stewart Home], Rick Gibson, Andy Hopton, Tom McGlynn and Stefan Szczelkun. "[The] show

can be seen as a continuous performance in which artists, objects, and audience, endlessly deconstruct and reconstruct 'glamour', a process which eventually results in the exposure of the mechanism underpinning this oppressive reification"- Karen Eliot.

305.
Savage, Jon. 'The Vague interview' and 'City 68/77/88/2000 towards a millenium'. *Vague*. (21), 1988, pp. 51-83.

Substantial interview with Jon Savage revolving around his work on the book *England's dreaming* [306]. The article 'City 68...' is a collage of items on The Mutoid Waste Company, Culturcide, millenarianism, and, in more detail, The Festival of Plagiarism.

306.
Savage, Jon. *England's dreaming: Sex Pistols and Punk Rock*. London: Faber and Faber, 1991. 602 p., ill. ISBN 0571139752.

More than just a history of the rise to fame of the Sex Pistols, Savage's book documents the condition of British culture in the late seventies. It also contains a good account of McLaren's and Jamie Reid's pre-Sex Pistols days. "I'd heard about the Situationists from the radical milieu of the time. You had to go up to Compendium Books. When you asked for the literature, you had to pass the eyeball test. Then you got these beautiful magazines with reflecting covers in various colours: gold, green, mauve. The text was in French: you tried to read it, but it was so difficult. Just when you were getting bored, there were always these wonderful pictures and they broke the whole thing up. They were what I bought them for: not the theory." — McLaren quoted p. 30. With an extensive bibliography and discography *England's dreaming* is also a useful reference tool for the period.

307.
The Spectacle. Self theory: the pleasure of thinking for yourself. *The Spectacle*. 2 (11) 1974. 13 p., ill.

Also revised and extensively rewritten by *Spectacular Times* as; *Revolutionary self-theory*. London: Spectacular Times, 1985. [24] p., ill. ISBN 0907837107. "This is a manual for constructing your own self-theory. Constructing your self theory is a revolutionary pleasure, the pleasure of constructing your self-theory of revolution." — Anon, p. [3].

308.

Stiles, Kristine. Sticks and stones: The Destruction in Art Symposium. *Arts Magazine.* 63 (5), Jan. 1989, pp. 54-60.

This article explores the connections and disagreements between the S.I. and The Destruction in Art Symposium organisers. "The historical irony of the absorption of the S.I. in academia is that artists [e.g. Metzger] whose social aims resembled theirs and with whom they contended in the 1960s, still remain outside critical discussion despite these artists' effort to create an aesthetic strategy that would insert their aims into the discourses of art and its history." — Stiles, p. 54. For more of the similar see; Stiles, Kristine. Synopsis of The Destruction in Art Symposium and its theoretical significance. *The Act.* (1), Spring 1987, pp. 22-31.; and *The Destruction in Art Symposium (DIAS): the radical cultural project of event-structured live art.* 1987. 3 volumes, ill. Thesis (Ph.D in History of Art) University of California, Berkeley, [Dec.] 1987. Bibliography: pp. 846-866. *Reference from OCLC.

309.

Tame, Chris R. *The politics of whim: a critique of the 'Situationist' version of Marxism.* London: Libertarian Alliance (1 Russell Chambers, London WC2E 8AA), [1991? revised edition of a 1975 publication]. 4 p. One sheet folded. ISBN 1870614291 (L.A. Pamphlet no. 9)

Excerpt from review in *Here and Now.* (11), [1991?], p. 33. "It comes as a surprise that a four-page leaflet could give a substantial critique of the Situationist project. It is all the more surprising that it could be based on a reading of 'Leaving the Twentieth Century' (always a strange and breathless selection) and written by an anarcho-capitalist." — p. 33. See also (or not); Tame, Chris R. *Unnecessary, unenforceable and unjust: a critique of bus smoking bans.* London: Forest, 1989. 12 p. ISBN 1871833078.

310.

Taylor, Paul, (ed.). *Impresario: Malcolm McLaren and the British New Wave.* New York; Cambridge, Mass.: New Museum of Contemporary Art and M.I.T. Press, 1988. 77 p., ill. ISBN 0262700352.

Catalogue of an exhibition held at the New Museum of Contemporary Art, Sept. 16 — Nov. 20, 1988. Contents: 'The impresario of do-it-yourself' by Paul Taylor, 'From Let It Rock to World's End, 430 King's Road' by Jane Withers, 'The great rock 'n' roll swindle' by Jon Savage, 'Malcolm McLaren and the making of Annabella' by

Dan Graham, and a 'Chronology' compiled by Malcolm McLaren [1946-]. For more on McLaren see; Bromberg, C. *The Wicked ways of Malcolm McLaren*. London: Omnibus, 1991. 330 p., ill. ISBN 0711924880.

311.
Totally Normal. *Oh no, I'm totally normal!* London: Totally Normal, [1990?]. [40] p., ill.
Narrative interspersed with détourned comics on the theme of work.

312.
Turner, Richard, (ed.). *Anti-clockwise.* (Liverpool) 1- 20, 1989 — 1991.
Consistently excellent 'pro-situ' photocopied fanzine. Articles on specific S.I. themes include 'Oh no, it's the situationists!' (3); 'Letter from Bruce Elwell' (4); 'Situationist theses on traffic' — Guy Debord (5); and 'How to have fun blowing things up: Meanings: Situationism' — Jack Shamash reprinted from *The Sunday Correspondent* (10). Closely connected with *Smile* and Art Strike circles, Turner now publishes *No* a similar project to *Anti-clockwise* (Information from; The Museum of Modern Alienation, P.O. Box 175, L69 8DY). Also by Turner; *In your blood: football culture in the late '80s and early '90s*. London: Working Press, 1990. 90 p., ill. ISBN 1870736079.

313.
Vague, Tom. The 20th century and how to leave it: the boy scout's guide to the Situationist International. *Vague.* (16/17), 1984 (second edition 1988), pp. 13-46. ISBN 1871692008.
An early attempt at an history of the S.I. concentrating on their possible influence on British pro-situ manifestations such as the Kim Philby Dining Club, the Angry Brigade, King Mob, Christopher Gray and Malcolm McLaren. Includes a bibliography.

314.
Vermorel, Fred, and Judy. *Sex Pistols: the inside story.* London: Omnibus Press, 1987. 239 p., ill. ISBN 0711910901.
First published in 1978 by; London: Star Books, 1978. 224 p., ill. ISBN 0426185854. See especially the chapter 'From Situationism to Punk', pp. 200-225, which recounts an anecdote about Debord's visit to London to inspect the troops and the introduction of McLaren to the S.I. "I [Fred Vermorel] returned to London [from Paris] with some

Situationist literature which fascinated Malcolm and which I translated for him. Jamie had meanwhile visited Paris as soon as he could after the events and made his own contacts with neo-anarchist and S.I.-influenced groups." — Vermorel, p. 222. This chapter did not appear in the 1978 edition.

315.
Walker, John A. *Cross-overs: art into pop / pop into art.* London: Methuen, 1987. 169 p., ill. ISBN 1851780157.

Notable for its list of Situationist techniques applied by McLaren to the Sex Pistols. "1) The construction of situations, that is, overcoming passivity, making things happen, introducing creativity and play into everyday life ... 2) 'Détournement' ... This technique was often applied by Situationists to the images and slogans of advertising. Reid's graphics for the Sex Pistols followed the same pattern ... 3) Never work, demolition of the work ethic ... 4) Society of the spectacle ... The Sex Pistols poured scorn on holidays in the sun and fast food products. They also encouraged the young to become producers of culture rather than consumers of it ... 5) Critique of bourgeois attitudes and values ..." — Walker, p. 120.

316.
Wicked Messengers. *Away with the murder of the body: can you feel anything when I do this?* London: Wicked Messengers, [1973?]. [16] p., ill.

Printed by Surburban Press. "It is an unauthorised transformation of a section from *Trois milliards de pervers: grand encyclopedie des homosexualities* by Researches, 73 Rue Buffon: 75005, Paris." — Wicked Messengers. Détourned film and television stills including 'Dirty Harry', 'Blazing Saddles', 'On the Buses', and 'Carry On films', arranged as a continuous comic strip. "However pseudo-tolerant it appears, the capitalist order in all its aspects ... continues to exercise over the whole desiring, sexual, affective life its totalitarian dominance, founded on property, male power, exploitation, surplice value." p. 1. Although the following item has no imprint details it looks very much like the work of Jamie Reid and Surburban Press; Anon. *Unbeatable self-defense.* [npl]: [n.d.]. [8] p., ill. A chiefly illustrated work with photo-collages and text concerning 'self improvement'. "No more leaders, no more experts, no more superstars, no more politicos, no more thinking that 'culture' can change anything except a few bank accounts." — p. [6]. This may have been an insert for another publication.

317.
Wilson, Andrew. Expresso Punk. *Art Monthly.* (154), March 1992, pp. 7-13, ill.
"Following the orgy of '60s nostalgia Andrew Wilson reviews the inevitable revival of interest in '70s Punk signalled by a clutch of new books on the subject." — *Art Monthly* editorial comment. These books are by Scott [137], Savage [306], and Bromberg [310]. The review contains an intelligent defence of Trocchi's "central position in the counter-cultural underground in the 1960s," and describes McLaren as Debordist. Includes a reproduction of the broadside distributed before the King Mob demonstration in Selfridges, *It was meant to be great but it's horrible,* 1968.

318.
[Wise, Dave.] *The end of music.* Glasgow: Box V2, 1978. 44 p., ill.
"Contents:- The revolution of everyday alienation, white dopes on punk, rebel music and state morality, music all day, helps you...work & play. The following article was written around 1978 and circulated in typescript form among people associated with *Solidarity* and *Infantile Disorder,* mainly in the Leeds area ... The original title was 'Punk, reggae; a critique.'" — p. 1. Unauthorised publication.

6. BOOK REVIEWS

6.1 Assault on culture [31]

319.
Ball, Edward. 'Possible worlds': the assault on culture from Lettrism to Class War. *Art & Text.* (Aust.) (35), Summer 1990, pp. 113-17, ill.

Positive review of Home's book. "Utopian art movements have been dramatically invisible since the heavy swing toward the pro-market ideology that accompanied the New York art boom of the 1980s. In our culture of amnesia, with its enforced consumption of all-new products, ideas, and texts, there is a *de facto* prohibition against historical consciousness. The *Assault on culture* serves as a post-mortem public relations tract for the underground, recording the labour of people who have lived their lives at a distance from institutions and the mainstream press, and placed themselves instead within the uncontaminated realms of word-of-mouth and popular memory." — Ball, pp. 115-116. Also includes a reproduction of the King Mob poster: *The death of art spells the murder of artists. The real anti-artist appears.* c. 1968.

320.
Black, Bob. Taking culture with a grain assault. [1990?]. 27 p.

Photocopy of typescript review of *Assault on culture* which was available in 1991 from Counter Productions, PO Box 556, London, SE5 ORL, England. A critical review of "Home's small-minded, mean-spirited screed" — p.27. Black berates Home for excluding utopian worthies (according to Black) such as American punks, hippies, yippies, Science fiction fans, Principia Discordia and other contemporary marginals. It accuses Home of being Eurocentric and only being interested in movements he has connections with, i.e. Punk and Neoism. Other critiques of *Assault on culture* by Black include; Black, Bob. [Review of the *Assault on culture*]. *Factsheet Five.* (USA). Summer 1989, (30), pp. 98-99; Black, Bob. *Beneath the underground.* Nashville: Conspiracy M.E.D.I.A., [1991?]; and Taking culture with a grain assault. *Black Eye.* (8), [1990], pp. 33-39. *References from Black, correspondence. Also circulated was a copy of Stewart

Home's 8 page reply to *Taking culture with a grain assault* which may still be available from B.M. Senior, London WC1N 3XX. "For me, the real challenge is to upset and infuriate a far broader section of the bourgeoisie than a clique of up-tight pro-situationists who are fixated on the idea (but certainly not the reality) of being 'revolutionaries.'" — Home, p. 8.

321.
Chernyi, Lev. Stewart Home's assault on coherent theory and practice. *Anarchy: a journal of desire armed*. (24), Mar./Apr. 1990, p. 6, + p. 8.
Critical review that tries to argue that Home puts "down the S.I. rather than genuinely coming to terms with it" but concedes that "it must stand as an ephemeral, interim study that will have to do until someone else does the job right." — Chernyi, p. 8.

322.
Dodson, Mo. Art Wars. *City Limits*. 6/10/88.
Short review. "Many of the absurdities perpetuated by these Utopian artists can be traced back to their naive belief in 'art' and 'real' desire, as if these were essentially the same thing in all human beings, and could be appealed to as panacea. While Home recognises that 'art' is a social construct, an invention of the Renaissance-Romantic period in Europe, he omits to apply the same analysis to 'desire'". — Dodson.

323.
Dunn, Lloyd. The assault on culture. *Photostatic*. (Iowa), (38), Oct. 1989.
Short review. "[Home] time and again points out how an awareness of one's history can provide practical benefits for making progress. The political views expressed are confrontational and pose a direct, rational challenge to power and those who wield it." — Dunn. Also in same issue, by same author, a review of the Festival of Plagiarism: Glasgow, Scotland, Aug. 4-11, 1989.

324.
Freedman, Ben. The assault on culture. *Border/lines*. (Canada), (15), Summer 1989, pp. 46-47.
Semi-critical review which perceives; "a failure to really discuss the problematic relation of culture to art in the bourgeois era ... I do think

Home is indulging in wishful thinking when he implies that art should be abandoned as an act of political conscience." — Freedman.

325.
McDonald, Angus (Third Assault). Not what it seems. *Here and Now*. (7/8), 1989, pp. 30-31.
A critical review of *The Assault on culture*. "In one sense Stewart Home has written a profoundly misleading book. The book presents itself as a basic introductory guide to its subject matter: utopian currents. It is nothing of the sort. It is polemic on two fronts. First an attempt to claim a heritage which can legitimate current art practices (including Home's own). Second, an attempt to specify within the heritage those elements to which he attaches the greatest importance." — McDonald, p. 30.

326.
Moore, John. Assault on culture: review. *Bulletin of Anarchist Research*. Feb. 1989.
"Rather than transcending the utopian tradition, Home constitutes its latest manifestation. In the Debordian terms which he despises yet assimilates, he realizes *and* suppresses the samizdat project." — Moore.

327.
Oldfield, Paul. Carnival time. *Melody Maker*. 17/9/88.
Short review. "We say that the only subversion left is refusing to constitute yourself, absenting from the battlefields where power and resistance keep producing each other: tune out, turn off, lapse from reality. Beside that *The Assault on culture* is a mausoleum of forms of resistance." — Oldfield.

328.
Oldfield, Paul. After the fall. *New Statesman and Society*. 12/8/88.
One page review of both *The Assault on culture* and *Apocalypse culture* edited by Adam Parfrey. "But there will be no millenium. Imagine instead the future according to Baudrillard ... where the social, political and cultural fabric has disappeared amidst non-participation, a refusal to reinvent power's networks." — Oldfield.

329.
Phillpot, Clive. Critical fictions: changing of the garde. *Artforum*. XXIX (2), Oct. 1990, pp. 33-35, ill.

> Phillpot suggests the time is ripe for a rehabilitation of the avant-garde. "By 'avant-garde' I meant art that was disruptive, subversive, oppositional, critical, challenging, even unacceptable, because of its appearance and because of its meaning; art that was not just a commodity — indeed art that might be impossible to own, let alone buy or sell." — Phillpot, p. 34.

330.
Suchin, Peter. Review of Stewart Home's Assault on culture. *Variant*. (6), 1988, pp. 21-22.

> Positive review commenting that this is an; "awkward area of research insofar as those groups and factions which flitted about the tricky interface of aesthetics and politics ... don't easily or directly coincide with the well-documented artworld entities such as Dada, the Surrealists, the Futurists and so forth." — Suchin, p. 22.

331.
Vague, Tom. Culturicide: review of Assault on culture. *Vague*. (21), 1988, pp. 87-94.

> An extended and humorous review and commentary on the book. Takes affront at the lack of any consideration of the Angry Brigade and the inclusion of Class War. On the S.I. Vague admits to being a Vaneigem fan. "Sure these people wrote a lot of bollocks when they got carried away ... That's what they did in the old student days. It can't really be taken directly today, in the context it was written at the time. But it does need to be criticised to give the would-be impersonators of today second thoughts." — Vague, p. 91.

6.2 Lipstick traces [42]

332.
Burn, Gordon. The power of synchronicity. *The Face*. 2 (9), June, 1989, p. 25.

> A brief review of *Lipstick traces*. "The Situationists believed in anonymity and evanescence; oblivion was there ruling passion. To the extent that, even though they were credited with shaping the

events of May '68 in Paris, they hardly existed themselves." — Burn, p. 25.

333.

Eagleton, Terry. Rotten, Vicious and Surrealist. *New York Times*. [no dates or page details].

"The metapolitical involves issues of desire, everyday life, the importance of microscopic gestures, which mainstream leftist politics has often enough breezily edited out. But it carries with it by the same token an anti-sociality that is impatient with institutions as such. It is hard to dismantle particular institutions without dreaming for a euphoric moment of what it might be like to be free of institutions altogether..." — Eagleton. For another short review of the book see; Strausbaugh, John. Never mind the bollocks, here's Mr. Marcus. *City Paper* (Baltimore).

334.

Herman, Andrew. You're under suspicion: Punk and the secret history of the 20th Century. In: *Version 90*. Allston, MA.: Steve LeBlanc, [1990]. ISBN 0941215067: pp. 72-91.

A Boston College sociologist recreats his own punk experiences in 1977 London with a critique of Marcus's secret history. "His ultimate stance in regards to the cultural politics of negation is basically that of a passive consumer rather than as an engaged critic or organic intellectual. He regards the events and personages of his secret history like he does the hundreds of recordings he probably receives each week for review: objects to be consumed, listened to, written about, and then filed away." — Herman, p. 90.

335.

Home, Stewart. A cosmetic underground. *Here and Now*. (10), 1990, pp. xiv-xv.

A critical review of *Lipstick traces*. "With the concept of the 'voice', a hidden authority which (dis)organises the world, Marcus abandons any need for a rational explanation of the events he describes. Such a mode of discourse has more in common with the simple faith of a priest than the considered reflections of a critic or historian..." — Home, p. xv. Different versions of this also appeared in; *New Art Examiner*. February 1990, p. 61.; *Smile* (11); and *City Limits*.

336.

McGann, Jerome. Umbah-Umbah. *London Review of Books.* 11 (12), 22 June 1989, pp. 13-15.

An affirmative review of *Lipstick traces* commenting on his historical structuring. " ... Marcus positively negates the great historical convention of narrative—not by avoiding narrative altogether (as in an almanac), but precisely by setting narrative(s) in motion and then running them all at each other along strange diagonals. The 'secret' of Marcus's 'history' is therefore its poetry, which appears most dramatically in the book's cut-up and paratactic structures." — McGann, pp. 14-15.

337.

Rogoff, Irit. Situations: tales of tiny epiphanies and radiant transgressions. *Art History.* 14 (1), March 1991, pp. 136-142. ISSN 01416790.

An extended review of *Lipstick traces* described as a "bold and intricate account of contemporary cultural history." "Marcus's argument is that one of the most potent gestures of cultural negation has been the myth of Dada, and thus his history of interventions, aimed at dismantling the very language of culture and guaranteeing against its reproduction, contains some unconscious echoes of that earlier movement within itself." — Rogoff, p. 140.

338.

Ross, Andrew. The rock 'n' roll ghost. *October.* (50), Fall, 1989, pp. 108-117. ISBN 026275200X.

A weighty, wide-ranging review of *Lipstick traces* which he describes as a genealogy of punk culture. "The given wisdom today, then, is that punk culture consciously invoked dadaism in its iconography and its 'bad attitudes', while its architects learned and successfully applied the situationist lessons about exploiting the media's hunger for spectacle." — Ross, p. 109. "In invoking the pop lyric of a 'new way of walking and a new way of talking' [Marcus] is trying to persuade us of the situationists' historical continuity with a cultural formation attuned to changes in the popular rhythm of events. But this cultural formation, in the realm of popular music, was simultaneously making its own history under conditions not at all of vanguardist making." — Ross, p. 117.

339.
Rumney, Ralph. Lipstick traces. *Art Monthly.* (30) October 1989, p. 31.
Short one page, generally positive, review. "There is one error on page 353 which needs to be corrected. There is no way the students union at the University of Strasbourg could have disposed of a budget of $500,000; if memory serves the figure involved was more like $1,500. " — Rumney.

7. 1989 EXHIBITION & CATALOGUE REVIEWS

The exhibition was organised by Peter Wollen and Mark Francis, with Paul-Hervé Parsy, in consultation with Thomas Y. Levin, Greil Marcus, and Elisabeth Sussman. A separate catalogue was produced for each show: Musée national d'art moderne, Centre Georges Pompidou, Paris, France, February 21, 1989 — April 9, 1989; Institute of Contemporary Arts, London, England, June 23, 1989 — August 13, 1989; Institute of Contemporary Arts, Boston, Massachusetts, October 20, 1989 — January 7, 1990.

340.

Ball, Edward. Welcome brigands. *Village Voice.* XXXIIII [sic] (18), May 2, 1989, p. 106., ill.

One page review of the Paris installation; "... the palpitations subsided and people came, some 1000 a day, the highest attendance figure for one Beaubourg exhibition in several years. And then the security guards chose early April, the last week of the show, to go out on strike, barricading the public out and themselves into the building." — Ball.

341.

Bonetti, David. The fizzled revolution: anti-art promised an explosion that never happened. *San Francisco Examiner.* 22/1/90.

One page review of the Boston installation. "The I.C.A. was unable to overcome the fact that it was the very kind of institution the S.I. most fervently opposed. Its installation tried to bring something of the street, the dérive into the gallery, but perhaps it should have thought about bringing the gallery out into the streets." — Bonetti.

342.

Bourriaud, Nicolas. The Situationist International: Centre Georges Pompidou, Paris. *Flash Art.* (146), May/June, 1989, pp. 122-123.

A brief equivocal review of the exhibition. "Few exhibitions have been so vital or ambiguous in recent years. Vital because the Situationist International is still rather unknown to the public, and also because the incendiary bombs launched by the S.I. between '57 and '62 have profoundly sustained subsequent generations [...] So, from whence does the feeling of malaise come, while visiting this after-the-event homage? Because all the S.I.'s critical enterprises can be read here as hollow, negative." — Bourriaud, p. 122. Article translated by Shaun Caley.

343.
Brenton, Howard. Showcase spectacles. *20/20*. May, 1989, pp. 24-26, ill.
Brenton relates how he blagged his way into the private view at the Pompidou. He also briefly mentions the use of Situationist techniques in his early plays such as 'Christie in Love'. "When I first read their strange pamphlets as a young playwright. I shouted for joy and ripped off what I took to be their ideas like crazy. I shamelessly 'co-opted' them to make plays ... Two of their 'techniques' interested me. There was 'détournement' which involves the deflection of ideas, objects, behaviour, from their accepted usage ... Then there was the technique of 'dérive' ... This was to set up 'situations' that are diverse, atmospheric, contradictory, which allows the spectator a mental freedom to wander about." — Brenton, pp. 25-26.

344.
Buck, Louisa. From the mundane to the ridiculous. *The Face*. 2 (9), June, 1989, p. 29, ill.
Brief discussion and recounting of familiar S.I. lore with little specific comment on the exhibition. "As early as 1959 the Situationists drew attention to the way in which the publicity industry exploited the language of modern art to dress up propaganda and entice the purchase of consumer goods. Through art the spectacle could be maintained." — Buck, p. 29.

345.
Core, Philip. Situation comedy. *New Statesman and Society*. 2 (56), June 30, 1989, p. 40.
Short one page review of the London installation. "While the entire undertaking is bound to provide a valuable critical reappraisal for forgotten work, it is also likely to provide a revelling in inappropriate heaviness and a veritable cyclone of hot air. Such are the inevitable concomitants of an attempt to describe art history as great because it is unknown, or works of art as influential because they happened to look like something else." — Core.

346.

Dannatt, Adrian. Sometimes a great notion? *The Times*. 21/7/1989, p. 21, ill.

This article sparked much discussion and controversy over the alleged links between Guy Debord and the C.I.A. These turned out to totally fictitious. Here is the significant passage. "Last month, in a leading *Village Voice* article [which did not in fact exist], it was revealed that Debord had been recruited by the C.I.A. in the very first years of the S.I., and had been receiving regular payments from its Parisian offices. This long-concealed information was only unearthed by chance during laborious research into American security information ... Expect anti-C.I.A. pickets at the I.C.A." — Dannatt.

347.

Danto, Ginger. l'Internationale situationniste: Centre Pompidou. *Art News*. 88 (9), Nov. 1989, p. 180. ISSN 00043273.

Concise, generally uninformative, commentary on the exhibition. "Situationism International [sic] (1957-72), according to the curators at the Centre Pompidou, was the last avant-garde movement of the 20th century. The statement is doubtless a way of labelling, for the purpose of this exhibition, an artistic movement that sought to elude definition." — Danto, p. 180.

348.

Frith, Simon. Situations and spectacle: making a mark. *City Limits*. June 15, 1989.

Two page review of the London installation. "The S.I. — whose organizational model was the spontaneous communist council, the eruption of pooled desire — can leave only the aesthetic spoor of its demands. The question, though, is whether one can go round their show without feeling the most debilitating of all left sentiments, that residue of all shocking art: nostalgia." — Frith.

349.

Hamlyn, Nicky. Those tricky Situationists. *The Guardian*. Tuesday 4/7/1989, ill.

"Can art change the world? Does the city control emotion? Do artists play into the hands of our political masters? For fifteen years, the Situationist grappled with these questions. Then in 1968 [sic], they

answered the last question with a 'yes' — and promptly disbanded."
— Hamlyn. It is also worth noting, briefly, that three short pieces appeared in the *Guardian* 'Notes and Queries' section on 5/8/91, in answer to the question 'Who were the Situationists?'

350.
Institute of Contemporary Arts [London]. [*The Situationist International talks*]. London : ICA, 1989. One sheet folded to provide a 10 page leaflet.
A leaflet produced to publicise various events scheduled to co-incide with the exhibition. Including information on the two day conference, 'Never mind the Bollocks, here's the Situationists', Saturday 24 — Sunday 25 June. Also lists a series of 23 films shown including 'The situationist life' by Jens Jørgen Thorsen and Jørgen Nash, Sweden (1963-66) and 'Situationisme n'est pas mort'; videos by Factory records and others. The I.C.A. also produced postcards and two t-shirts as marketing spin-offs. These t-shirts carried the 'Situationist' slogans "One has only to pick at the scab of memory, and the cries, words and gestures of the past make the whole body of power bleed again" and "The point is not to put poetry at the disposal of the revolution, but to put the revolution at the disposal of poetry."

351.
Institute of Contemporary Arts [Boston]. *Symposium on the Situationist International* 1957-1972.
Flyer to advertise the event that occurred on October 21, 1989. Speakers were Mark Francis, Elisabeth Sussman, Peter Halley, Hal Foster, Thomas Y. Levin, Greil Marcus, Jim Miller, Susan Suleiman, and Peter Wollen. The program: 'Historical background and formulation of the S.I.', 'The context of S.I. artistic and political practice', and 'The S.I. influence on contemporary culture'. The museum also produced a small flyer/catalogue for the show that has this quote from Bernstein; "I shall break the good news. Any 'core of five or so' people — some of them with jobs, some of them selling paintings, like Asger Jorn — can produce a wonderful review like Internationale Situationiste [sic]. There is no mystery. A review with no office, no staff — where all the work, typing, lay-out, proof-reading, is made by the unpaid collaborators, and which appears at intervals from six months to one year, is not that expensive. And if the 'core of five' involved do not spend the little money that they

have on other things, like the ones on which some other people put their dreams, nice clothes, cars, sunny holidays, hi-fi chains... if they joyfully accept to be, most of the time, rather broke, there is no problem. So if any group of five to ten people do not produce a review like Internationale Situationiste [sic], it is not the funds which are lacking; it must be something else." — Bernstein, p. [6], 1989.

352.
Lubbock, Tom. Situation comedy. *The Independent*. Tues. 4/7/89, p. 14.
"Tom Lubbock is unshocked by the Situationists and stimulated by Bridget Riley's eye for colour."- *Independent* editorial comment. Review of London installation

353.
Mull, Robert. On the passage of a few people through a rather brief moment in time: the Situationist International 1957-72. *AA Files*. (21), Spring, 1991, pp. 108-109. ISSN 02616823.
A text which discusses what he perceives as the failure of the Branson Coates design for the I.C.A. installation. He goes on to criticize the show for its; "obsession with the artefacts at the expense of the political circumstances that had shaped them."- Mull, p. 109. Only ostensibly a review of the Sussman [57] catalogue. "In failing to realize the potential of the work of the S.I. to inform contemporary events, the exhibition organisers may unwittingly have returned it to obscurity."- Mull, p. 109.

354.
Phillips, Christopher, Homage to a phantom avant-garde: the Situationist International. *Art in America*. 77 (10), Oct. 1989, pp. 182-191 (+p. 239), ill. ISSN 00043214.
More than a review of the exhibition, this article is a general introduction to familiar issues. Phillips describes the S.I. as a "thriving cottage industry" [of which this bibliography is a participant and a witness]. It also contains a short inserted article on 'The invisible films of Guy Debord'. "[Wollen] sees the Situationist movement as the final curtain call that closed the era of the 20th-century avant-gardes — an era begun with Futurism in 1909 and continued through Dada, Constructivism and Surrealism. To examine seriously this idea of the end of an era in which formal artistic experiment and

radical cultural critique went hand in hand would be a provocative step, to say the least. The present exhibition does not go so far." — Phillips, p. 239.

355.
Salvioni, Daniela. Sur le passage de quelques personnes à travers une assez courte unité de temps. *Arts Magazine*. 63 (10), Summer, 1989, p. 105.
A critical review of the exhibition. "Part of the problem with the situationist show is the absence of any effort to contextualize the movement historically ... By presenting situationism in a historical vacuum, by gliding over its glaring failure to assess adequately the events themselves as they were happening, the movement becomes the stuff of aesthetic *flâneurs*, making this exhibition a missed opportunity."

356.
Sewall, Brian. Creating a stink. *Evening Standard*. London, 13/7/89, p. 29.
A short critical review of the London installation. "It is the contemptible expression of our age that had nothing but contempt for beauty, and believed that it could replace art in which it had no faith with social and cultural definitions. Far from vigourous, intelligent and substantial, its subversive ideas were spiteful, silly, morbid and pretentious, and we suffer from them still. The exhibition ends in a sludgily painted chamber, the air mephitic with a stink that induces violent hay fever; the catalogue is bound in sand-paper- 'That' said the vendor with Situationist malevolence, 'is meant to ruin your other books'". — Sewall.

357.
Sinker, Mark. Open cities. *Marxism Today*. July 1989, p. 43.
"Situationism, the doctrine of a clique of French artists and intellectuals who disbanded in the early 70s, continues to hold a strange fascination. Mark Sinker weighs up its impact and its teen-appeal." — editorial. Short review of the exhibition.

358.
Smith, Peter. On the passage of a few people: Situationist Nostalgia. *Oxford Art Journal.* 14 (1), 1991, pp. 118-125. ISSN 01426540.

An intelligent and quite comprehensive critical review of Blazwick [11] and Sussman [57]. "My view of the exhibition and these complimentary texts is that they seem for the most part to lack the critical motivation and the dialectical irony of the Situationists. They are normative representations, reverential in tone, recuperative in effect and the ideological positions which they reflect are conveniently distanced from those of the S.I." — Smith, p. 118.

359.
Soutif, Daniel. l'Internationale situationniste 1957-1972. *Artforum.* 27 (9), May 1989, p. 165.

A short semi-critical review. "The [exhibition] came up against a multiplicity of difficulties, not the least of which was the attempt to museumize a movement that saw art, and even more so the museum, as old hat and to be buried as quickly as possible. To see the Situationist pamphlets today, primly displayed under Plexiglas, is unintentionally comic... To have exhumed situationist works without attempting to place them in perspective would have been even more suspect. We might as well smile at this unavoidable paradox without any further attempt to analyze it." — Soutif, p. 165. Article translated by Hanna Hannah.

360.
Suchin, Peter. Rebellion remodelled. *Here and Now.* (9), [Summer 1990], pp. 14-15.

A ambivalent review of both the exhibition and the conference 'Never mind the Bollocks, here's the Situationists'. "To take the situationists seriously is to realise that their critique of 'everyday life' is by no means 'out of date'. It is not a fashion item. Nor is it any kind of desolate regression to look back at work some thirty years old, as long as one's view is not merely an exercise in nostalgia." — Suchin, p. 14.

361.
Vague, Tom. Sur le passage de quelques personnes à travers une assez courte unité de temps. *Vague*. (22), 1990, pp. 3-6. ISBN 1871692024.

An account of Vague's trip over to Paris for the opening of the show. Short account of the show itself although there is more on the socialising. "[A] complete set of IS's on a table under glass—not as flash as you are lead to believe, but it would have been nice to flick through them—everything being under glass makes it seem like they're historic relics, which wasn't supposed to have happened, was it?" — p. 4.

362.
Waintrop, Édouard. Détournement de situs par les beaubourgeois. *Libération*. Feb. 24, 1989, pp. 32-34.

Said to contain a statement by Paul-Hervé Parsy, the Beaubourg curator. "We are quite aware of the paradox but in an art world where the word simulacrum is on everyone's lips, where Jean Baudrillard is so often cited (especially in the U.S.), we wanted to return to the sources, to the Situationists' reflections on the society of the spectacle." *Reference from Phillips [354], p. 189.)

363.
Wilson, Andrew. Sur le passage de quelques personnes à travers une assez...: L'Internationale situationniste, 1957-1972. *Artscribe*. (77), Sept/Oct. 1989, pp. 89-90., ill.

A critical review of the Paris installation particularly on the blurring of the differences between the 2nd International, formed in 1962 and the Debord/Vaneigem Situationist International. "This split which cast the Situationists into two different camps is barely expressed in this exhibition save by the realisation that there are fewer pictorial objects on show and more books and pamphlets to be seen ... mere cultural icons and nothing more than the surface of appearances ... The intention is quite obviously clear: the institutional cataloguing of the Situationist programme as a Situationism that is museum-ready for public consumption..." — Wilson, p. 90. Wilson also quotes Debord; "The end of cultural history manifests itself on two opposite sides: the project of its supersession in total history, and the organisation of its preservation as a dead object in spectacular contemplation. One of these movements has linked its fate to social critique, the other to the defence of class power."

SELECTED ADDRESSES

A Distribution, 84b Whitechapel High Street, London E1. [1992]
AK Press, 22 Lutton Place, Edinburgh, Scotland, EH8 9PE. Phone/fax (031) 6671507. [1993]
Against Sleep Against Nightmare, P.O. Box 3305 Oakland, CA 94609. [1988]
Ann Creed, 22 Cecil Court, London WC2N 4HE. [1993]
Aporia Press, 308 Camberwell New Road, London SE5, UK. [1988]
Artcore Editions, Weisestr. 58, 1000 Berlin 44, Germany. [1993]
Art Strike Action Committee, P.O. 170715, San Francisco, CA 94117. [1990]
Autonomedia, POB 568, Williamsburgh Station, Brooklyn, NY11211-0568 USA. [1992]

Black & Red, P.O. Box 02374, Detroit, MI 48202. USA. [1991]
Black Mask, P.O. Box 512, Cooper Station, New York, NY USA. [1968]
Blast, Box 27, c/o 31 Manor Row, Bradford, West Yorkshire. [1991]
B.M. Combustion, London WC1N 3XX. UK. [1987]
Bratach Dubh Editions, BCM Box 7177, London. UK. [1990]
Bureau of Public Secrets, P.O. Box 1044, Berkeley, CA 94701. USA. [1992]

Capitalist Crisis Studies, P.O. Box 754, Berkeley, CA 94701. [1977]
Caribbean Situationist, B.M. Box Soon, London WCIV 6XX. [1973]
Centre de Recherche sur la Question Sociale, B.P. 218, 75865 Paris CEDEX 18. [1976]
Chronos Publications, London WC1N 3XX, UK. [1990]
Compendium, 234 Camden High Street, London NW1 8QS. [1993]
Council for the Liberation of Daily Life, Box 666, Stuyvesant Station, New York, NY 10009. [1968]
Counter Productions, P.O. Box 556, London SE5 ORL. UK. [1992]

Diversion, P.O. Box 321, 542 Atlantic Avenue, Brooklyn, NY 11215. [1973]
Drift Distribution, 219 E. 2nd Street #5E, New York, NY 10009. [1993]

Éditions Champ Libre, 6, rue des Beaux-Arts, 75-Paris. [1972]
Éditions Gérard Lebovici, 27, rue Saint-Sulpice, 75006 Paris, VI. [1990]
Edition Nautilus, Verlag Lutz Schulenburg, Hassestr. 22-2050 Hamburg 80, Germany. [1990]

Elephant Editions, B.M. Elephant, London WC1N 3XX. UK. [1990]
Encyclopédie des Nuisances, 74 rue de Menilmontant, 75020 Paris, France. [1990]

Fifth Estate Books, P.O. Box 02548, Detroit, MI 48202. USA. [1991]
Flatland, P.O. Box 2420, Fort Bragg, CA 95437-2420. USA. [1991]
For Ourselves, Council for Generalized Self-Management, PO Box 754, Berkeley, CA 94701 & PO Box 745, Palo Alto, CA 94302. [1974]
Freedom, 84b Whitechapel High Street, London E1. [1993]

Galerie 1900-2000, Marcel Fleiss, 8, rue Bonaparte 75006 Paris. [1989]
Galerie Nane Stern, 25, avenue de Tourville, 75007 Paris. [1984]

Here and Now, c/o Transmission Gallery, 28 King St., Glasgow G1 5QP or Here and Now, P.O. Box 109, Leeds, LS5 3AA. [1992]
Housman's, 5 Caledonian Road, London N1. [1993]

Inland Book Co., P.O. Box 120261, East Haven, CT 06512. [1991]
l'Institut de Préhistoire Contemporaine, B.P. 20-05, Paris. [1972]
The Institute of Contemporary Art, 955 Boylston Street, Boston, MA 02115, USA. [1989]
International Institute of Social History, Anarchism Department, Herengracht 262-266, Amsterdam. [1976]

Last International, 55 Sutter St. 487, San Francisco, CA 94108, USA. [1987]
Left Bank Distribution, 4142 Brooklyn N.E., Seattle, WA 98105. [1991]
Libertarian Book Club, 339 Lafayette St., Room 202, New York, NY 10012. USA. [1991]
Libertarian Alliance, 1 Russell Chambers, London WC2E 8AA. [1991]
Lightworks Magazine, P.O. Box 1202, Birmingham, MI 48012-1202, USA. [1992]
Loompanics Unlimited, P.O. Box 1197, Pt. Townsend, WA 98368. USA. [1991]
Lure Art Books, 2215-R Market St., No. 315, San Francisco CA 94114. [1993]
Lutwidge, Charles, P.O. Box 1503, Palo Alto, CA 94302, USA. [1976?]

Marginal Distribution, Unit 103 Lower Mall, 277 George St. N., Ontario K9J 3G9 Canada. [1991]

Museum für (Sub-) Kultur, Fuldastrasse 33, 1000 Berlin 44. [1979]
Museum of Modern Alienation, P.O. Box 175, Liverpool, L69 8DY. [1992]

National Art Library, Victoria and Albert Museum, South Kensington, London, SW7 2RL. [1993]
The Negative and its Use, P.O. Box 5025, Berkeley, CA 94705, USA. [1976?]
News From Everywhere, Box 14, 136 Kingsland High Street, London E 8. [1988]
Not Bored! PO Box 3421, Wayland Sq., Providence, RI 02906. . [1992]

Online Computer Library Center, 6565 Frantz Road, Dublin, OH 43017, USA. [1993]
Officini Edizioni, Passeggiata di Ripetta 25, Rome, Italy. [1977]

Pelagian Press, BCM Signpost, London WC1N 3XX. UK. [1992]
Pending Press, Box 99, 234 Camden High Street, London NW1. UK. [1992]
Pirate Press, P.O. Box 446, Sheffield, S1 1NY. UK. [1991]
Pleasure Tendency, P.O. Box 109, Leeds, LS5 3AA. [1986]
Polygon, 22 George Square, Edinburgh. UK. [1991]
Point-Blank, P.O. Box 2233, Station A, Berkeley, CA 94702 . [1974]

Rebel Press, 84 b Whitechapel High Street, London E1. UK. . [1992]
Researches, 73 Rue Buffon: 75005, Paris. [1973?]

Sabotage Editions, B.M. Senior, London WC1N 3XX. UK. [1992]
Sam Fogg, Rare Books and Manuscripts, 14 Old Bond Street, London, W1X 3DB. [1991]
Shix-flux, Smile, Box 3502, Madison WI 53704, USA. [1988]
Shutes, Chris. P.O. Box 4502, Berkeley, CA 94704. [1983]
Silkeborg Kunstmuseum, Gudenavej 9, Postboks 940, DK-8600 Silkeborg, Denmark. [1988]
Small Press Distribution, 1814 San Pablo Ave., Berkeley, CA 94702. [1991]
Social Revolution, Box 23, APP, 167 King St. Aberdeen, Scotland. [1978] and Box. 217, 142 Drummond St. London N.W. 7. [1978]
Spillers of Seed, 789 2526 Hillsborough St. Raleigh NC 27607. USA. [198?]
Spontaneous Combustion, Box LBD, 197 Kings Cross Road, London WC1. [1974]

Unpopular Books, Box 15, 136 Kingsland High Road, Dalston, London E8 2NS. UK. [1992]

Up Against the Wall Motherfucker, 341 E. 10th St. New York, NY. [1968]

Upshot, P.O. Box 40256 San Francisco, CA. (earlier) and Upshot P.O. Box 26135 Los Angeles, CA. 90026 (later). [1975]

Urban Morphology Research Group, School of Geography, University of Birmingham, B1S 2TT. UK. [1991]

Vague, BCM Box 7207, London, WC1N 3XX, England. [1992]

Wicked Messengers, BM Box Salt, London, WC1V 6XX. [1972?]

Yawn, P.O. Box 227, Iowa City IA 52244, USA. [1993]

INDEX

145

Some Recent Titles from AK Press

WHICH WAY FOR THE ECOLOGY MOVEMENT? — by Murray Bookchin; ISBN 1 873176 26 0; 80 pp two color cover, perfect bound 6 x 9 £4.50/$6.00. Bookchin attacks the misanthropic notion that the environmental crisis is caused mainly by overpopulation or humanity's genetic makeup. He points to the social and economic causes as the problem the environmental movement must deal with.

TO REMEMBER SPAIN — by Murray Bookchin; ISBN 1 873176 87 2; 80 pp two color cover, perfect bound 6 x 9 £4.50/$6.00. Bookchin places the Spanish anarchist movement of the 1930s in the context of the revolutionary workers' movements of the pre-WWII era.

IMMEDIATISM by Hakim Bey; ISBN 1 873176 42 2; 64 pp four color cover, perfect bound 5-1/2 x 8-1/2; £4.00/$6.00. A new stunning collection of essays from the author of *TAZ: Temporary Autonomous Zone*, beautifully illustrated by Freddie Baer.

TESTCARD F: TELEVISION, MYTHINFORMATION AND SOCIAL CONTROL constructed by Anonymous; ISBN 1 873176 91 0; 80 pp four color cover, perfect bound 5-1/2 x 8-1/2; £4.50/$6.00. Using savage image-text cut and paste, this book explodes all previous media theory and riots through the Global Village, looting the ideological supermarket of all its products.

END TIME: NOTES ON THE APOCALYPSE by G.A. Matiasz; ISBN 1873176 96 1; 320 pp four color cover, perfect bound 5-1/2 x 8-1/2; £5.95/$7.00. A first novel by G.A. Matiasz, an original voice of slashing, thought provoking style. "A compulsively readable thriller combined with a very smart meditation on the near-future of anarchism, *End Time* proves once again that science fiction is our only literature of ideas." - Hakim Bey

No PITY by Stewart Home; ISBN 1 873176 46 5; 144 pp two color cover, perfect bound 5-1/2 x 8-1/2; £7.50/$11.00. With this collection of nine short stories, Mr. Home gives fiction back the bad name it deserves.

STEALWORKS: THE GRAPHIC DETAILS OF JOHN YATES by John Yates; ISBN 1 873176 51 1; 136 pp two color cover, perfect bound 8-1/2 x 11; £7.95/$11.95. A collection to date of work created by a visual mechanic and graphic surgeon. His work is a mixture of bold visuals, minimalist to-the-point social commentary, involves the manipulation and reinterpretation of culture's media imagery.

AK Press publishes and distributes a wide variety of radical literature. For our latest catalog featuring these and several thousand other titles, please send a large self-addressed, stamped envelope to:

AK Press
22 Lutton Place
Edinburgh, Scotland
EH8 9PE, Great Britain

AK Press
P.O. Box 40682
San Francisco, CA
94140-0682